First Grade Writers

Stephanie Parsons

First Grade Writers

Units of Study to Help Children Plan, Organize, and Structure Their Ideas

Foreword by Katie Wood Ray

HEINEMANN
Portsmouth, NH

Heinemann
361 Hanover Street
Portsmouth, NH 03801–3912
www.heinemann.com

Offices and agents throughout the world

Library of Congress Cataloging-in-Publication Data
Parsons, Stephanie.
    First grade writers : units of study to help children plan, organize, and structure their ideas / Stephanie Parsons.
        p. cm.
    Includes bibliographical references.
    ISBN 0–325–00524–9 (alk. paper)
    1. English language—Composition and exercises—Study and teaching (Primary).
2. First grade (Education).   I. Title.

LB1528.P27 2005
372.62'3—dc22   2005009954

Editor: Kate Montgomery
Production: Lynne Costa
Cover design: Night & Day Design
Typesetter: Technologies 'N Typography
Manufacturing: Jamie Carter

Printed in the United States of America on acid-free paper
09 08   RRD   5

For my friends and colleagues at the Teachers College Reading and Writing Project, with love and gratitude

Contents

Foreword

I asked Stephanie Parsons a few years ago if I could write this foreword, before the book even existed as anything more than an idea for a book. This is not how forewords are supposed to come to be. First of all, the author of the book really should do the asking, so I was perhaps a little—shall we say—*forward* in soliciting this one for myself. And I swear, I don't normally go around asking for foreword-writing jobs. It's just that I wanted to write this one because I so wanted Stephanie to write this book. I loved her thinking, and I wanted to learn from her what she knew about teaching young children. I wanted her voice to be heard in the larger conversation about the teaching of writing that is carried on in professional books about this topic. And I trusted her thinking about teaching enough to solicit this foreword spot before the book was even written. I'm so glad I did.

There are many things to love about this book.

For me, the love begins with the title: *First Grade Writers.* The clear, declarative stance of the title is also the stance of this book. Stephanie Parsons believes that the children who come into her workshop in first grade are *writers.* Not writers-in-waiting or writers-to-be or even beginning writers. Just writers. This belief, that there is not some threshold of development children must reach before they can be thought of as writers, is clear in everything Stephanie writes about, from planning to teaching to assessment. I believe readers of this book will love the clarity of this stance.

I also love the details. In the introduction to *First Grade Writers,* Stephanie says, "Details alone do not improve the quality of writing. In fact, they can detract from that quality." And while she's talking about writing when she says this, I couldn't help but think about how this is also true of teaching. So often we teachers *crave* the details. We think if we could just get our hands on the book lists and lesson plans and writing supplies of the teachers we admire, if we could just get our hands on more *details,* we could improve the quality of our teaching. But, in fact, more details in our teaching can detract from its quality if we don't also have a "big-picture" understanding of why those details matter and how they came to be.

Readers will love that this book both offers the big-picture understandings of the teaching and zooms in and looks at the details of that teaching. Stephanie begins by explaining her goals for the year: to help children grow in the areas of writing quality, writing habits, writing conventions, and community. Then she zooms in a little more closely and lets us see what that growth would look like in each area; for example, one of the writing habits is that children will "read published books not only as readers but also as writers."

As the teaching unfolds in each chapter, Stephanie returns to these same four goals over and over and explains how the different units of study are designed to support children's growth in each area. I believe the artfulness in her teaching is found in the sameness of her design. With her structured teaching design thus made transparent, Stephanie offers readers many precious curriculum details referred to as "possible teaching points." In every study, she shows us a range of the kinds of things she might teach (curriculum) and a variety of ways she might teach them (instruction). I also love the respect she shows for her readers by sharing teaching possibilities rather than teaching directives.

The role of immersion in quality literature is a theme across the book. The planning for each study begins with Stephanie showing us the texts she has collected to read to children so they will have a vision for the kind of writing she wants them to do. Readers will love that she shares titles of texts, but even more, they will love that she opens up some of her thinking about why she has selected these particular texts. She also includes examples of the kinds of things she and her students have learned from the authors of these texts, giving readers an insider's look at the kind of curriculum generated when young children are taught to look at texts through a writer's eyes.

Readers will love the examples of children's writing spread throughout the book and the very thoughtful assessment rubrics Stephanie has designed to look at this writing and the writers who stand behind it. Readers will love the honesty with which Stephanie acknowledges problems that might occur in each study and the practical solutions she offers as possibilities. And readers will love the accessibility of Stephanie's teaching, the easy way she invites us into her thinking and makes this teaching seem so real and so possible.

There is just a lot to love about this book.

I actually knew *about* Stephanie Parsons before I knew her. Some years ago my good friend and colleague, Isoke Nia, was working as a staff developer in Stephanie's room and she kept telling me, "You should see this teacher, Katie, this classroom. They sing all the time. Good songs, too. Folk music, old Motown. And you should see their writing. It's an incredible place. . . ." Isoke's enthusiasm made me long to meet Stephanie and see her classroom. I believe that readers of this book will feel the same longing I did and will be thankful that we now have this book through which we can meet and see.

—*Katie Wood Ray*

Acknowledgments

I have the good fortune of belonging to rich communities of teachers, writers, and artists. Everything I accomplish is with the support and inspiration of friends.

Katie Ray provided the motivation to write this book. I am deeply indebted to her for sharing her wisdom and encouragement.

The Teachers College Reading and Writing Project community is the source of my learning and the life of my teaching. I am grateful and honored to know the people who make up this organization. Lucy Calkins challenges me to do better every day and supports me as I try. I am a better teacher because of her. Laurie Pessah always has the most practical advice. Her example has kept me sane through a year of writing this book while working full-time. Kathy Collins, a brilliant teacher, writer, staff developer, and friend, has been a touchstone of calm. Just being around her is joyful. Mary Ehrenworth has opened my eyes to new ways of seeing my work. Kathleen Tolan always has a kind word when times are tough. Amanda Hartman, a friend as much as a colleague, is a generous and gifted collaborator. Colleen Cruz showed me that I really could finish my book. Each of my fellow staff developers has been a fertile source of good ideas. The kind and capable support staff makes my work richer and certainly easier.

Isoke Titilayo Nia has opened my eyes to so much about writing and about children. Loving yet demanding, she has lifted my practice and my confidence. From Isoke's fellow staff developer, Gaby Layden, I learned so much about narrative writing. I also owe Carl Anderson many thanks for his ideas about writing stories.

I had the privilege of working in a school filled with amazing teachers. Liz Phillips and my colleagues at P.S. 321 created an environment of rigorous and joyful learning. My work was made richer by the contributions of some incredible parents and children.

In schools all around New York City, and in Los Angeles, Kansas City, White Plains, and Fort Worth, I have met and collaborated with some of this country's most thoughtful and creative teachers, administrators, and children.

Hilary Liftin read parts of this book and asked me the best questions. She is a great writer and a great writing teacher.

Kate Montgomery, my editor and friend, is a fantastic reader. She has a special gift for suggesting changes that make exactly the most sense. She has kept this process fun for me, which is perhaps the most important contribution of all.

Frank Zizzo is my source of sanity.

To my family, my first reading and writing teachers, I am thankful for everything.

Christina Kelly kept me writing but also knew when I needed to step away. Her inspiration and support are great treasures.

I owe all of these people the warmest gratitude.

Introduction

Underneath almost everything we do or make is some sort of structure. We may not be able to see it, but it is there, holding everything together. Behind our walls are studs, beneath our floors are supports, and beyond our ceilings are joists; without them, our houses would not be able to stand. In much the same way, structure allows us to communicate ideas. How would you tell someone what it means to be a teacher? Would you start saying whatever came into your mind in random order? Probably not. Instead, you would first think of the parts that together create a complete picture of teaching. You might make a list of each important aspect and then go back and elaborate on them one by one. You could tell a story that would illuminate who you are as a teacher by choosing to include certain details and events and exclude others. Behind these decisions would be your knowledge that you must communicate your thoughts within a structure so that your audience can better understand them.

When children first come to school, they have lots of ideas to share and stories to tell. Most young children tend to communicate these things in a stream-of-consciousness manner, saying whatever pops into their heads. Their writing often sounds like their speech. In Figure I.1, Sarah tries to tell a story about visiting her grandmother, but it ends up sounding like a to-do list. Her readers do not get a sense of why this story is important or what was meaningful to her about the visit.

However, some clear teaching of structure helped Sarah focus her story on just one part of her visit and elaborate on that part so her audience could understand why it mattered. This time when we read the story (see Figure I.2), we

One day I went to a store in Saranac where my grandma lives and when we got inside I saw some marbles and we bought them and then we bought some soap and a coloring book and some cleaners and some groceries and then we went on line and then we went home and got our bathing suits and went to the pool for an hour and then we went home.

FIGURE I.1 *Sarah's Grandma Story Before Structure Work*

laugh or nod in recognition of the sentiment Sarah is expressing. By using a narrative structure that helps her be both more specific and more descriptive, she makes her story really reach us.

For years I thought that if I told my students to add details to their writing, I could get them to say more about their topic, tell more interesting stories, or convey information more clearly. Mostly what they did, however, was add more words, usually to the end, without adding clarity or substance. Details alone do not improve the quality of writing. In fact, they can *detract* from that quality. I needed to teach children how to start a piece of writing with a plan in mind and then to add to that writing only those words or details that would help fulfill the plan.

WHEN I got HOME I FRUND ON THE
TV and some THING BAD WAS ON
50 I chachD THe CHAhL and agen
and agen and rHen FINLY I Found a
GOOD show ON DISNY and I was Relr
Relr! HUNGERY and THeN FINLY IT
WAS DINNer TIme and I RUShT
TO THe COUNTER and RUShT
BACK and saT DOWN and ATE and
WReN THe FRST SKOOP went INto MY MOUTH
I paRtly FAINTED

When I got home I turned on the TV and something bad was on so I changed the channel and again and again and then finally I found a good show on Disney and I was really really! hungry and then finally it was dinner time and I rushed to the counter and rushed back and sat down and ate and when the first scoop went into my mouth I partly fainted.

FIGURE I.1 *(continued)*

This book is about teaching children who are just learning how to write to plan and organize their ideas as they communicate them. The concept is introduced using simple text structures like pattern books and question-and-answer books. During the year, students build up to the more complex structures needed to write personal and fictional narrative. Throughout the process, they develop the habits and skills of organizing ideas, planning how their work will go, and using structure to communicate clearly.

Goals for the year are divided into four categories: writing quality, writing habits, writing conventions, and community. These goals take into account not only children's ability to structure text but also my belief that classes must be communities and children must become independent if they are

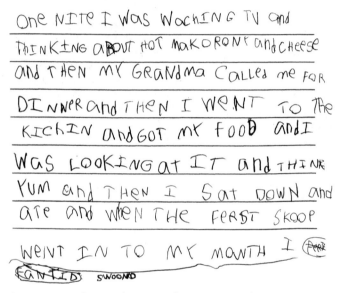

One night I was watching TV and thinking about hot macaroni and cheese and then my grandma called me for dinner and then I went to the kitchen and got my food and I was looking at it and thinking yum, and then I sat down and ate and when the first scoop went into my mouth I swooned.

Figure I.2 *Sarah's Grandma Story After Structure Work*

going to write authentically and from the heart. In a nutshell, these are my goals:

1. **Writing quality.** Children will:
   - Write pieces that seem complete: they provide enough information and none that is extraneous.
   - Think about which words to use to say exactly what they mean.
   - Include description or elaboration that supports the overall meaning of their writing.
   - Explore ways to make time move more slowly in their narratives:
     - ❏ Describe the internal thought processes of a character.
     - ❏ Tell events in greater detail.

- Explore ways to make time move more quickly in their narratives.
- Show events happening (through dialogue, for example), not tell about them.
- Show emotions, not tell about them.

2. *Writing habits.* Children will:
   - Read published books not only as readers but also as writers.
   - Begin to think about why an author has made certain decisions in his or her writing. (For example, they might examine the effect the writing has on them as readers.)
   - Try to achieve desired effects by using techniques they see in published books.
   - Revise their work as they write, whenever they write, not only during lessons concentrating on revision.

3. *Writing conventions.* Children will:
   - Put spaces between words consistently.
   - Use correctly formed letters of the correct case.
   - Use periods, question marks, quotation marks, and exclamation points correctly.
   - Correctly spell about one hundred frequently used words.
   - Use known words to find the correct or nearly correct spelling of unknown words.

4. *Community.* Children will:
   - Make informed decisions about which peers to ask for help with certain aspects of writing.
   - Demonstrate a knowledge of and interest in their classmates' writing.
   - Treat the learning environment with respect; that is,
     - ❏ Take care of tools and supplies.
     - ❏ Be conscious of the noise level.
     - ❏ Be mindful of other writers' time and space.

I am often amazed by the things first graders are able to accomplish. The teachers and children I have worked with have achieved impressive results by focusing on structure as part of their writing curriculum. I hope these units help you do just that and that I have left room for you to find your own voice inside them. Certainly, they do not represent all the work that goes on in a writing workshop. Other units of study, perhaps from the series Units of Study for Primary Writing, by Lucy Calkins and the Teachers College Reading and Writing Project, can be used to develop additional writing skills. Figure I.3 is a possible

MONTH	UNIT
September	Building Community
October	Pattern Books
November	Nonfiction Question-and-Answer Books
December	Small Moments
January	Author Study/Revision
February	Revision/Writing for Readers
March	Nonfiction All-About Books
April	Poetry
May	Personal Narrative
June	Fiction

Figure I.3 *Possible Calendar for Writing Workshop Units*

calendar of how these units can work together. You may also teach these units within your mandated curriculum or as part of established themes.

The units of study I describe in this book are those I find most helpful in developing children's abilities to plan, organize, and structure their ideas into comprehensible and complete pieces of writing. Every unit is presented in the same way: I start with a brief overview and then discuss in more detail how I plan and teach the particular unit. The planning steps are outlined below.

■ Setting Goals

Limiting the goals of a given unit of study can be difficult. I want to teach everything at once so that my kids can do it all, right now! And that's why this step is so important. I *can't* teach it all at once. I have to set goals for each unit that are realistic and that build on the work of prior units so that I have taught everything I need to by the end of the year.

I have driven across our country from one coast to the other a number of times. Each of these journeys was different, but they all had one thing in common. Each time, my companions and I decided on a specific destination and date of arrival and a general route and time frame. We were aware that unforeseen circumstances could cause us to change roads or spend more or less time in certain places. We may have had to go north for a few days to get west. We may have known that we were definitely going to visit Chicago or New Orleans, but we were free to decide on other stopping points as the spirit (or a flat tire or an oil change) moved us. Each leg of the journey was important in its own right, but all the legs worked together to get us to the final destination.

A year of writing workshop happens pretty much the same way. I have my eyes on our final destination, but I focus on the daily steps that will move us ever closer to it. I keep a map handy the whole way so that I can respond to the specific needs of a class of individual children with thoughtful teaching that will keep us going in the right direction. Every unit has a smaller and more manageable set of goals that will move us forward to the end of the year, and the choices I make on my feet are guided by these intermediate goals.

■ Getting Ready to Teach

Before beginning a new unit of study, I need to prepare for the curriculum physically and mentally. I gather the materials I will need (including *mentor texts*, models of good writing in a particular genre using a particular structure) and think about what lessons will be best to teach. I reflect on the unit that came before, looking at how I guided my students toward those goals and planning how I will continue to guide them toward the next set.

Considering the Students

I use student work to assess not only the children's accomplishments in the unit they are finishing but also what they need to learn in units to come. Their published pieces and the daily writing that accumulates in their folders tell me what I need to do in my lessons and conferences in order to facilitate their progress.

Published work tells me how students shape a piece of writing. I learn how much ownership they take of their writing and how they use writing and revision strategies. I look at this work with questions in mind about the writing and about the writer:

- Did this child love this piece of writing, or did she choose it for publication just because it was getting close to our celebration date?

- Do I hear his voice in this writing? Does it seem as though he developed the work according to his own ideas?

- Is there evidence that she made changes—are there carets, cross-outs, additions? What kind of changes did she make—single words, whole sentences, entire pages added or removed, spelling changes, wording changes?

- Did his revisions make the piece more focused, clear, and complete or less so?

- Has she corrected spelling and punctuation she has learned since the piece was first written?

The rest of students' work needs to be considered just as thoughtfully. The daily writing that builds up in their folders reveals their automaticity, writing habits, willingness to take risks, and comfort with new skills and strategies. I look at this work with different questions in mind:

- Does he try new kinds of writing or new topics? Does he have a favorite topic to which he returns often? If so, does he write about it in the same way, or does he try to approach it differently in new pieces of writing?

- Does she make changes to the writing as she goes?

- Does he return to writing? Does he have any ongoing projects, such as a book or a long story?

- Does she seem to have fun? Does she seem to want perfection? Does this help or hurt?

- Does he use new skills or spelling words I have taught? Can I read the writing better than I could last time I looked? Has his use of conventions improved?

Gathering and Studying Books

Each unit requires a number of books that will become mentor texts for the children and teaching aids for me. Of course, I may refer to other books, but I need a core set of books to which I can return again and again as I teach the skills and qualities of good writing. The strong, clear qualities of good writing in the books I choose are the examples that teach children how to develop those same qualities in their own writing. A great mentor text contains lots of teaching possibilities.

After I gather a set of books, I must read them all carefully, looking for possible teaching points. Having a good understanding of what mentor texts have to offer gives me a greater vision of what my students can do. I am no longer bogged down by that old standby "Add details." A single book may contain examples of how a writer chooses words to create mental images, uses punctuation to build tension, and includes dialogue to help the reader feel part of the story. I decide which of these many qualities to teach based on the purpose of the current unit of study and the readiness of my children to learn. For example, I don't need to teach children how to use dialogue in a nonfiction unit or when they are still using a few simple sentences to tell a story. I keep sticky notes inside each book on which I write the page numbers of good examples of quality writing. I use these examples to

- *Plan lessons.* I look for examples and ideas that relate to the particular unit and to the children's needs.

- *Prepare for conferences.* Twenty or thirty children have about as many needs. One student may need to see an example of a certain way to organize questions and answers, another may need a book from which to do some research, and a third may need to see a variety of ways to break away from a habitual format.

- *Prepare for small-group work.* Often an example that benefits one child will also benefit a few others. I gather a small group of children and use multiple copies of the book or an enlarged copy of a given page or passage to teach the strategy or technique.

As I conduct individual lessons or conferences, I rely on the sticky notes to lead me to clear examples of each writing skill or strategy I teach. I may not use every single example I have identified, but when I need to change direction a little, I'm prepared.

Providing the Right Paper

Having the right paper can make a big difference in children's writing development. I can invite a child to say more about a topic by putting more lines on the paper. I can let him know that his picture is an important ingredient of his story by giving him lots of room for it. Each unit contains examples of paper layouts that can support children in meeting the goals of that unit.

■ Dividing the Unit into Sections

Each unit is divided into the same sections (with the occasional variation). A consistent daily schedule helps children accomplish more. Predictable components let children get better at *studying* writing as well as at writing.

Reading Like Writers

I begin each unit by having children read the kind of books they are going to be writing. Knowing the books well as readers lets them read the way a writer might, by looking at the author's craft—how he uses words and punctuation, how she put her book together. *Wondrous Words,* by Katie Wood Ray, and *Authors as Mentors* (from the Units of Study for Primary Writing series), by Lucy Calkins and Amanda Hartman, are fantastic resources on the craft of writing.

Writing with Intention

Writing has a purpose and an audience. It is meant to communicate an idea. Children need to discover that their voice matters, that learning to write well serves their purposes, not the teacher's. I want to support their needs and their growth, not help them do better on an assessment. When children consider their audience, they are motivated to write their ideas clearly and explicitly and to attend to conventions. When they take the initiative, they look inside themselves for the messages they want to send, choosing topics and genres that support their needs. The beauty is that most children who have a vested interest in their writing lives *do* perform better on standardized assessments.

Revising the Writing

Revision applies to all writers, not just adults or older children. Children choose the piece of writing (or pieces if they are short or the child has extra time) they think best represents their growth as writers and learn a new strategy for revising them. The strategy then becomes part of their repertoire of writing skills. I used to think of revision as making writing *better,* but I now suggest a more helpful and friendly definition: *Revision* is the act of making the writing more closely match the writer's ideas and feelings. It can be as simple as adding a smile to a face in a drawing to make the emotion clearer. When I went to school, I thought I had to revise my writing because it wasn't good enough the first time around. Now I tell children they need to revise their work precisely because it *is* good enough. Good writing deserves to be revised. "Bad" writing is also an important part of the process, but it might not merit a lot of extra labor. When children are taught to write and revise at the same time, revision becomes much less of a chore.

Editing

Put simply, editing is what children must learn to do to make their writing readable. Editing may mean putting spaces between words, using more letters (or the right letters) to represent the sounds in words, correcting spelling and punctuation, or making sure all of the intended words are written on the paper. As soon as children are writing (or approximating) words, they can learn to edit. Each unit includes a suggested editing lesson, but only you will know which editing strategy is appropriate for your class at any given time. If your class is just starting to write words, it may not be appropriate to expect the students to use periods and capital letters correctly. It may be better to teach them to read their writing by following it with a finger, pointing under each word. Whatever strategy you choose, it is important to get children looking at their work critically and thoughtfully.

Reflecting on What Has Been Learned

As children share their work during and at the end of a unit, I encourage them to reflect on what they've done: What have they learned? What do they think they have done well? What was difficult for them? What do they wish they had done better? This helps me determine whether I am getting my point across and see how my adult teaching is being translated into the children's language. More important, it encourages children to find words to describe what they are learning to do as writers. When they can name their intentions, it becomes possible for them to judge for themselves whether or not they are successful. Their writing and revising are now motivated from within, not by me.

Publishing and Celebrating

Now that their work has been revised and edited, it is ready for some final sprucing up. This could mean giving it a pretty cover, coloring the illustrations nicely, writing a dedication, telling readers about the author, or adding a blurb to the back cover. The idea is that when they send their work out into the world, children make it more special than all the other work that stays in the folder. They are ready to celebrate! This is their reward for all their hard work.

A celebration for each published piece of writing (say, nine or ten a year) may seem overwhelming, but not every celebration has to have balloons and parents and cupcakes. Most, in fact, are simple and intimate: gathering in a circle and sharing favorite pages, complimenting each writer as his or her writing is posted on the bulletin board, or making a toast with a cup of juice, congratulating their achievement as you launch them into the next challenge. Of course, one or twice you'll want to pull out all the stops and invite the children's families and the school community to share in the joy and pride that comes from a job well done.

Don't skip this step. Even a small celebration is important to the future of a writing community. A celebration at the end of a unit of study is like a graduation. Children acknowledge and validate the progress they have made by naming the new skills they have mastered or at least begun to master. They also prepare mentally for a new unit, an unknown territory into which they can venture with the certainty that all their efforts will be rewarded with new learning. Celebrating is a way to become aware of learning, and it helps children undertake the work more fearlessly than they otherwise might.

Building a Community of Writers

1

Before we can teach first graders how to turn their thoughts into nicely structured pieces of writing—before we can teach them much of anything—we must first establish a community of learners. The writing children do during a school year requires them to be active participants in their learning. You do not want merely to walk them through the eight or ten or twelve pieces of writing they will publish in a year, giving daily assignments to the whole class. Instead you want to teach them useful skills and strategies so that they can make many more pieces of writing independently. You need to foster the attitude that you are all in this together. You need to be a community.

In a community of writers, children

- are willing to take risks and try new things

- want to write every day

- see their daily writing as something that benefits them (rather than as something you want from them)

- cooperate in maintaining a productive environment

- may be working on different kinds of writing at different paces from one another

- know and care about what their classmates are working on

- listen to one another's writing

- comment thoughtfully on one another's work

- value one another's efforts

When we speak of building a community of writers, we acknowledge our students as individuals with a shared purpose. And what better shared purpose for a community of writers than to express our thoughts and beliefs, feelings and hopes in the most clear and organized way possible?

■ Overview

This unit of study, which prepares the class to learn how to plan, organize, and structure a piece of writing, takes about four or five weeks. *Launching the Writing Workshop,* by Lucy Calkins and Leah Mermelstein, the first in the Units of Study for Primary Writing series, is an excellent resource for September writing workshop minilessons. As well as teaching children about writing, you need to direct your energy toward building the community, setting up routines, and making your expectations for student behavior clear.

Start by establishing writing workshop as something you do every day and that everyone *can* do. In the first week or two of school, have an informal celebration to signify that everyone is indeed a writer. Move on to teach children that writers care deeply about their work. Then focus on the habits writers need to develop. Finally, teach about revision and editing, introducing checklists for each.

Throughout the whole unit, you'll want to alternate between three kinds of lessons: those that address writing quality, such as how to come up with a topic; those about routines, such as how to get to and from the meeting area; and those about community, such as how to comment thoughtfully on a classmate's writing. None of these types of lessons exists in a vacuum; they need to be taught together in order to create a complete writing workshop: one that runs well, benefits the students, and feels like a safe place to take risks.

■ Goals

You'll have distinct goals for the whole year, some that will be reached in a given unit and others that will be approached in the various units and reached by the end of the year. This unit is different from the rest because it involves laying the foundation on which all of the teaching that follows will be built. You are fertilizing the ground so that all the teaching you do during the rest of the year can take hold and grow into something fabulous. You can teach amazing lessons, but if the class does not function well in the workshop setting, your efforts will not yield amazing results. The goals for establishing a strong writing community that will last the whole year fall into three categories.

Building Community

Children will:

- Listen to one another's work and ideas.

- Show respect for everyone's work regardless of its level of achievement.

- Understand that one's physical ability to write is not directly proportional to the writer's intelligence or to the quality of the writing.

- Comment on others' work respectfully and thoughtfully.

- Listen to, read, and discuss literature together.

- Savor words together.

- Be familiar with core books.

- Tell and value stories from their shared or individual experiences.

- Show enthusiasm for writing.

Writing Habits

Children will:

- Pay attention (both to the teacher and to each other) and participate in minilessons.

- Participate in and follow up on conferences.

- Move around the classroom quietly and responsibly.

- Carefully get and care for their own supplies.

- Work quietly for increasingly longer periods of time.

- Help themselves and one another so as not to interrupt conferences.

- Use the classroom as a resource for spelling, writing ideas, behavior reminders, and support.

- See writing possibilities everywhere (even at recess!).

Writing Quality

Children will:

- Choose topics that matter deeply to them.

- Try a variety of genres or forms in their writing.

- Understand that writing is meant to be read and has the job of communicating something to its audience.

- Think of themselves as writers with messages.

- Develop and maintain a daily habit of writing quietly.

- Return to pieces of writing on subsequent days.

■ Getting Ready to Teach

There is so much hope and anticipation inherent in opening a fresh box of markers or unwrapping a brand-new pack of colored paper. We say to ourselves, "This year is going to be great. I am so much smarter about teaching than I was a year ago." And it's true! Every year we get to decide anew how best to organize our room for the massive amount of reading, writing, observing, discussing, and problem solving that is going to happen there.

In looking at your goals for September, you need to imagine the kind of world you are going to create in your classroom so that children can be successful. Children will follow you toward these goals only if they feel safe and valued when taking the kinds of risks and responsibilities required. The way you set up the classroom environment, rules, routines, and rituals will have a major impact on how safe and valued your students will feel.

Of course, you'll introduce new rules and routines a little at a time, as the children are ready for them. Yet the more you've thought them through on day one, the more smoothly you'll be able to bring the class on board.

Environment

The classroom needs to be set up to foster independence, even though at first you will do many things for the children that they will eventually learn to do for themselves and for one another. You'll have a writing center stocked with some tools and supplies, with room to add others as children learn to use them. In the beginning, there may be just pens or pencils, paper, and date stamps. In time, you'll add tape, scissors, sticky notes, white correction tape, and several types of paper.

The meeting area is an important part of the environment, a place where the children gather for minilessons and sharing. You'll need an easel or stand of some sort so that you can demonstrate most of what you teach.

Finally, there needs to be space to hang children's writing publicly—a bulletin board or a section of the chalkboard. You may also want to set aside wall space where you can display students' amazing language or other great things they've attempted.

Rules

While it helps the sense of community to set up rules for writing workshop with input from the children, you need to begin with some idea of what you want these rules to be. There should be only four or five, and they should be connected to your rules governing other parts of the school day. This way, you can reframe their childlike suggestions to fit your vision of writing workshop. For instance, if a child suggests a "No talking" rule, you can rephrase it as "When we talk in writing workshop, we'll talk about our writing." Other important rules may address how children speak about one another's work, how they use their time in writing workshop, or whether or not they may leave the meeting area during a minilesson or sharing session.

Routines and Rituals

Before children set foot in the classroom you need to imagine many of their routines. Will they get folders and pencils individually, or will a monitor do so for the entire table? Will they write with pencils or pens? How will they get to and from the meeting area? You can't expect children to learn the routines smoothly unless you have a clear idea yourself of what they are.

Rituals are equally important. What parts of a writer's life are worthy of special ceremonies? Obviously, finishing a unit of study and publishing the work created is one, but you will want to identify others. These may be small, such as welcoming a new book into the library the first time you read it aloud, or large, such as inviting the whole school to hear the children read their poems in the garden. Other important occasions may be the first day of a unit of study, telling a shared story orally, putting a new word on the word wall, changing writing partners, and so on.

■ Teaching

In September, we must do whatever it takes to get children personally invested in learning, sharing, and taking risks. For that to happen, they must experience success. Children take cues from the behavior of the adults that matter in their lives. If we talk about community ideals but act as though we are really the ones who control the classroom, children learn to talk the talk without necessarily walking the walk. We have to mean it when we tell them their voices and ideas matter. I went into teaching because I was secretly (or not so secretly, according to reliable sources) a control freak. It was hard to give up many of my great ideas in favor of allowing the class some say in how our year would go or what our rules and routines would be or even the direction of our curriculum. My reward for letting go was the satisfaction of a class that spoke thoughtfully (and quite impressively) about their learning.

I am not advocating anarchy nor fostering a spirit of anything goes. (I hear my fellow control freaks exhaling a sigh of relief.) If we commit to giving children real responsibility in the life of the classroom, we must teach them, clearly and explicitly, how to use that responsibility. Several lessons at the beginning of school must be about how, if we are going to have the privilege of writing workshop, we have to work together to create and maintain a time and place for it that is precious—to everybody. You can divide these lessons into sections that will be steps along the way to a smoothly running and cooperative writing workshop.

To some extent, *when* you teach certain lessons depends on your particular needs. For instance, I cannot stand having conferences interrupted, so during the first week of school I teach children how to take care of themselves when I'm having conferences with their classmates. On the other hand, while I do not like looking at ragged corners of children's precious writing peeking out of the sides of their folders, I can ignore it for a while. We all have our priorities. If papers protruding from your students' folders are going to drive you crazy, by all means teach children how to put paper into a folder the correct way as soon as possible.

Other lessons are not as flexible. The first day of writing workshop, for instance, has to be what Isoke Nia, an inspiring speaker and brilliant teacher of teachers, calls "the love day." Before my students hear about how to sit and be quiet and take care of their pencils and paper, before they hear about choosing a topic, I want them to hear about how great writing is, how lucky we are to get to do it together every day, how much we're going to learn, and what a privilege it is to be able to teach them about something that matters so deeply to me.

Looking back over my plan books for the last few years, I see a pattern of lessons in September roughly like the one shown in Figure 1.1.

Though it may seem that children have an awful lot of responsibilities here, not all of them need to be taught in a minilesson. Some can be addressed by interrupting the workshop with quick instructions as needed; and some, like keeping the room quiet, may not need to be *taught* at all. Children know how to work quietly. However, you do need to make sure they know how important it is to keep the room quiet and help them become personally invested in doing so. You can do this most effectively by reminding them often to keep the noise level low (you may start to feel like a nag, but you won't have to do it for long) and praising them when they do.

We Are All Writers

We want to communicate to children in every way we can that we are going to become a community of writers. And our actions *are* going to speak louder than our words. We cannot simply tell children, "OK, guys, we're a community now, so we're all going to write every day and love it." It's got to be much more delicate than that. The best way to get children to want to write every day is to make it something at which they often succeed. We all enjoy doing things we are good at. We especially enjoy being complimented on things we have worked hard to accomplish. It takes the pleasure out of almost anything when somebody constantly critiques our performance without giving any positive feedback. When I have a conference, I might notice several things the child needs to work on. Rather than immediately point these things out, I do myself a favor by gushing a little over his effort: "Wow, Alex! Look at what you've done here!" When a child who usually stares at a blank page, refusing to pick up a pencil and claiming to have no ideas, makes a tiny scribble on his paper, I behave as if I'm throwing a party: "Oh, William, this is a big day for you! I'm so excited I can barely wait to see what you make!" When a child who already identifies herself as a failure at age six throws her crumpled drawing into the trash, I pull it out, making a big show of smoothing and caring for it: "Emily, I'm sad you thought you made garbage today. Let me show you how precious it is."

At the end of this week, it makes sense to have a quick publishing celebration. Publishing children's writing, hanging it up on the wall, and toasting one another with plastic cups of juice are easy ways to give the class a big dose of feeling successful and proud and to encourage the budding sense of community. The writing also provides a good assessment of students' habits and attitudes as writers and tells you what they need to learn.

TIME (A GENERAL GUIDELINE)	SECTION OF STUDY	WHAT NEEDS TO BE DONE IN THIS SECTION? *CHILDREN WILL:*
4–6 days	We Are All Writers	• Write every day. • Be able to get started without being told what to do. • Use pictures to tell stories well. • Learn routines for getting to and from the meeting area. • Get their tools and supplies independently. • Treat their tools and supplies with care. • Keep the classroom quiet. • Learn some ways to work productively so that they do not say, "I'm finished," or interrupt conferences. • Realize that they can write different kinds of things (such as cards, books, or lists). • Publish a piece of writing.
4–6 days	Writers Tell the Stories That Matter Most	• Choose topics that are close to their hearts. • Choose small topics. • Plan stories before writing them. • Use pictures and words to tell their stories. • Spell words by saying them slowly and writing down the sounds they hear. • Learn to use ABC tape or chart to help with spelling. • Learn to add on to a piece of writing from another day.
4–6 days	Writers Have Routines	• Plan sentences before writing them. • Learn how to comment productively on one another's work when they share. • Learn how to manage ongoing work in their folders. • Start every workshop by looking at what is already in the folder. • Learn how to behave in conferences.
2–4 days	Writers Revise and Edit	• Become familiar with the concept of a revision checklist by being introduced to one item (adding to a piece of writing). • Become familiar with the concept of an editing checklist by being introduced to one item (making sure there are spaces between the words).
2 days	Reflection and Assessment (with Publication)	• Choose two pieces to publish. • Celebrate their completion of the unit of study.

Figure 1.1 *Building Community at a Glance*

Possible Teaching Points

- *Writers treat their tools and supplies with care.* Teach children not just to treat classroom supplies well but also to care about treating them well. Communicate to children that the tools and supplies belong to *them,* not to you.

- *When writers think they're finished, they read what they just wrote, read another piece of their writing, or start a new piece of writing instead of saying, "I'm finished," or interrupting a conference.* It isn't fair to ask children not to interrupt conferences without teaching them how to keep themselves occupied productively during writing workshop. If they have options for how to use their time, children will learn to become more independent.

- *Writing takes many forms, like books, cards, songs, signs, instructions, and letters.* Teach children the many ways they have for getting their ideas across. Showing them examples of all these kinds of writing (and more) lets them see what they, too, can accomplish as writers.

- *Writers think of an idea that matters enough to write a lot about it.* Many children need specific help getting started each day. When a child learns to choose topics that engage him as a writer, he builds stamina and independence. In your conferences, steer children toward engaging topics. Look for facial expressions and vocal inflections that indicate enthusiasm.

- *Writers use pictures to help tell their stories well.* Early in the school year, children have a great deal more to say than they can physically write down in a single workshop. Pictures contain information about the setting and the people in the story and can help them remember ideas from one day to the next. This not only helps them write more about each idea but also supports ongoing projects.

Writers Tell the Stories That Matter Most

In preparation for deeper work on text structure during the year, we need to teach children how to find great ideas for writing inside themselves and to write about them with focus. These qualities are the first building blocks of a well-organized piece of writing. We want children to think more deeply about what they are putting onto their papers. You may have already told them that writers choose to write about the things that matter most in their lives. This week, go further and teach them how to focus their writing on a small topic (not "my trip to Florida," but "when Grandma and I went hunting for shells"). Also teach them that writers reread their work often and sometimes add information. They will start using pictures and words to tell their stories, which will require some strategies for spelling, such as using a word wall or alphabet chart or tape.

Possible Teaching Points

- *Writers choose topics that are close to their hearts.* This concept has already been addressed briefly. Work more deeply and thoughtfully to help children think about what really matters to them. It may help to frame questions such as "When I read your writing, what do you need me to know about you?" or "What are the stories that have made you who you are?"

- *Writers choose small topics.* Focus is essential to good writing. While there are other ways to focus a piece of writing (on a theme, a concept, a place, etc.), a concrete way to teach this concept to young children is through the idea of small moments or events. A child's story about walking down the hall to her classroom by herself for the first time is going to be more engaging than a litany of all the things she did at school that day. In conferences, you might say, "Can I help you find and write about the most important part of that whole day?"

- *Writers can add words below their pictures or to the lines of text they've already written.* You've already taught how to tell stories well with pictures. Now demonstrate using the detailed information in drawings to inform the writing: "When you told me about your story, you said your mom tied your shoes. I see that here in the picture but not down here in the words. Can I help you add it?"

- *Writers can add labels to their pictures.* Sometimes writing a sentence or two below a picture can be a big project for a child. In his enthusiasm to get the whole idea onto paper, he may let his use of conventions slip, making the piece difficult to read later. Thinking about conventions when writing a single word is much more manageable, so teach students that they can put labels into their pictures. When they write the labels, they can put more attention into saying each word slowly and writing the letters that represent the sounds they hear.

- *Writers add to pieces of writing they worked on before.* It's not enough to tell children to go back through their folders and find pieces to which they can add. Teach them how to do this in a thoughtful and meaningful way, not going back to all pieces of writing or just any piece of writing, but rather revisiting pieces that show promise. Teach them to look at a piece of writing and ask, "Do I have more to say about this idea? Does this story make me feel excited to say more?"

- *Writers spell lots of words by saying them slowly and writing down the sounds they hear.* You have implicitly demonstrated saying words slowly as you wrote down ideas in earlier lessons. Now demonstrate explicitly how this process works. Say the word not once but several times, listening to different parts. Then show students how to reread the word when they finish writing it and how to reread the whole sentence each time they add a new word.

- *Writers use details from a story in their pictures.* Some children need help adding important elements of an oral story into their drawings. Teach them how to retell their stories, one part at a time. As they tell each part of the story, have them check the picture to see whether anything needs to be added.

- *Writers add details from a story to their words.* Teach students to reread their words to see if any new information needs to be included.

- *Writers plan their stories before they write them down.* Sometimes children tell the best stories and then write something completely different. They may have forgotten how their oral version of the story ended or may have been distracted by another memory. Help them get from the oral to the written version with a simple planning technique: Give them either stapled booklets of three pages or paper divided into three sections (legal size works best here). Then teach them to rehearse for writing by touching each page or section as they say what will be written on that page. This helps children remember what they wanted to write on the third page even if the first two pages take a long time to finish.

Writers Have Routines

You've already taught many behavior-related routines. Now you're ready to teach more sophisticated ones. Children need to learn how to comment on one another's work in a way that helps the writer. They need to know that a writer can do several things to be productive: go back through the folder to look for ideas worth developing, start a new piece, draw a picture of an important time in her life, write about an idea she has written about before. They also have to become fearless spellers. I almost never tell children how to spell words during

rkshop. (Child: "How do you spell *summer?*" Me: "I listen to the
y slowly and write them all down. Let me teach you how." It's not
she wants, but it's the response she needs.) In word study, I tell
spell many words, but in writing workshop they must fend for
ing the strategies I teach. All these things enable children to con-
ndependently when I am conferring with other writers.

.. Teaching Points

- *Writers plan a sentence before writing it down.* You model this important
  skill every time you write something in class, but some children may require
  explicit teaching. Show children how to say ideas out loud before writing
  them down. Point to each spot on a line where a word will eventually go.
  When writing the words, think aloud about how you are writing the words
  on the paper exactly where you touched it when you said them aloud.

- *Writers work together to maintain a productive environment.* Instead of
  teaching children how to *do* something, teach them how to *be aware* of what
  they do. Working together to maintain a productive environment means
  working quietly, treating tools and supplies with care so they last a long time,
  trying the strategies that have been taught in minilessons, sharing ideas with
  peers, listening to their ideas, being willing to take risks, and supporting others as they take risks. All of these things require some awareness and effort.
  When you demonstrate these kinds of behavior, children have an example to
  follow.

- *Writers get ideas for their writing from other books.* Teach children to notice
  and try techniques and skills that published authors use. Introduce the idea
  by reading a book aloud and demonstrating how to write a similar one.

- *When sharing (or during peer conferences), it is more helpful to make comments about a writer's process than about content.* During a writing workshop, the students help you teach. When handing them the responsibility
  (and privilege) of giving and receiving comments, you must also teach them
  how to make comments that really help the writer. You will build on this skill
  for months, but you can start early. Make the distinction between saying, "I
  like your picture," and saying, "I like how all of the important information
  from your story is right there in your picture."

- *Writers have strategies for staying productive when they feel like doing something else.* This is more likely taught in a conference than in a lesson because

individual children have individual needs relative to building their stamina. Possible strategies include going back into their folders and looking for unfinished work, taking a quiet walk around the room to look at what other children are doing, looking at a favorite book, or looking around the room or out the window to see if anything sparks a memory. (In dire circumstances, point out that recess comes only once a day. If a student takes recess during writing workshop, he'll have to write when all the other children are taking *their* recess.)

- *Writers learn from their mentors.* Even this early in the year, some children are ready to look to mentors for ideas. In a conference, show how to notice how a writer uses words, puts ideas together, or uses other crafting techniques. A conference like this can become a great minilesson the next day in which you use the student's writing as an example of how to learn from a published book.

Writers Revise and Edit

Every unit of study includes a period of revision and editing before publishing. This is part of a writer's routine and it should become part of children's lives as writers. At this point, children's folders should be bursting with attempts at and approximations of different kinds of writing. Some papers may contain a few scribbles and jumbled ideas. Others may be readable stories, lists, or other bits and pieces. It is important to remember that even writing that doesn't seem very good or readable is an important step toward becoming a stronger writer.

From all of this work, have children choose one or two pieces that represent their best work and learning during the month. Teach them how to use revision and editing lists (and add new strategies to these lists near the end of each unit). Since a list like this is a new concept, I usually make the first items strategies I've already taught them. This way, they don't have to learn to use the checklist and brand-new strategies at the same time. For example, in this unit a revision strategy could be adding to a piece of writing and an editing strategy could be making sure all words have spaces in between them.

Possible Teaching Points

- *Using a revision checklist: Writers can revise by adding to their work.* Embed teaching how to use a revision checklist within teaching the revision strategy. Demonstrate how we can add information or ideas to any piece of writing.

- *Using an editing checklist: Writers make sure their words have spaces between them.* If children are still forgetting to put spaces between all their words, teach them to go back and add slashes or dashes to make the writing easier to read. Not all children will need this strategy, so you may decide to make this a small-group lesson or conference rather than a whole-class lesson. Again, show the children an editing checklist that contains the strategy.

- *Good writing deserves to be revised.* Many children do not like to go back to their work once they feel it is finished. Cajoling and persuading don't seem to work: they think it's good just as it is. Try telling children that revision is what happens to good writing, not something we do to make our writing better: "Of course it's good as it is! That's probably why you chose it as the piece to publish. Now that you have it picked out, you're ready for the next step!"

- *Writers don't bother to revise writing they don't like.* Sometimes a child chooses to publish a piece of writing to which he doesn't seem to have much connection. Perhaps he thinks it's something you want him to publish. Help the child go through his folder again, watching his face for signs of enthusiasm as he revisits his work. It takes time for some children to develop a deep connection to what they write. Helping them understand that what they put onto paper is a reflection of who they are can support their whole writing lives.

Reflection and Assessment (with Publication)

This is the first major publication of the year, so you'll want it to be particularly rewarding for the children. You'll also want it to be intimate. This is a chance for you to get to know one another even better and to celebrate the distance you have traveled in this short amount of time. Therefore, hold off on inviting parents and other classes. Instead, share juice and a small snack as you walk around the room looking at everyone's writing, which should be carefully laid out on desks. After this, gather the class near the writing bulletin board and tack each new piece into place. As you do so, invite the writer to comment about the piece or say one thing she or he has learned so far in writing workshop.

■ Predictable Problems

No matter how complete our planning, how pure our intentions, how deep our knowledge, how great our experience, or how energetic our approach—no matter what—there will always be problems. Our job is not to teach without trouble but to recognize and respond to that trouble effectively. Some problems are impossible to predict, but others are easy to imagine. The following list is not complete. Your students may present challenges I haven't mentioned. If so, try to imagine how you might deal with them. Also remember that we undoubtedly become frustrated from time to time. The way we approach difficulty will resound in the hearts and minds of our students for a long time. I try always to remind myself that my job is to help children solve their problems in a way that makes them feel loved and successful.

PROBLEM	WHAT IT LOOKS LIKE	POSSIBLE SOLUTION/ CONFERENCE
Children lack confidence or are afraid to take a risk.	• Children write about the same topic you used in the lesson. • Children write what seems to be the same book over and over. • Children write only the words they know how to spell. • Children stare at their papers but do not write anything.	It is especially important to compliment children who lack confidence. Be on the lookout for things they do well, because they will know if your compliment is authentic. Remind them of some of the things they know and care an awful lot about. They might not realize how much they know!
	• Children discard pieces of writing with only a few words or a tiny drawing on each page.	Teach children to value all their attempts. Also teach them about process: if they make mistakes, they can continue working on the same piece of paper. Doing this with kindness and understanding helps children be willing to take ever bigger risks.
	• Children distract others by talking or making noise.	When fear of taking a risk looks like a behavior problem, it is tempting to chastise, but it's better to encourage.
Children choose uninteresting topics.	• Children choose the same topic over and over.	Many writers return to a few topics often throughout their careers. It is not necessarily a bad thing when children do the same. They will move on when they are ready.
	• Children seem to be writing about things that have no importance to them.	Children have many important stories to tell. Sometimes these are hidden within or disguised as mundane accounts. Instead of suggesting other topics, help them get at the heart of what they are trying to say. If you don't tell them you believe their stories are important, how will they know?

PROBLEM	WHAT IT LOOKS LIKE	POSSIBLE SOLUTION/ CONFERENCE
Children don't internalize routines.	• The classroom remains noisy. • Children laugh, chat, play, distract others, or wander around the classroom during writing workshop.	Make sure you include children in the process of setting up routines. Don't tell them to be quiet because *you* want it quiet. Rather, ask them what *they* need in place to help them learn and grow as writers. When they tell you they need the room to be pretty quiet, agree to help them achieve this: "You were so clear that you wanted a quiet space to work in, so I'm happy to stop you as many times as I have to in order to help you get the room exactly how you want it to sound."
	• Children speak disparagingly about one another's work.	Model often how you want children to comment on writing. Tell the class when you see a child respond to another's work in a helpful or kind way.
Your teaching is not reaching all learners.	• More advanced students do not appear to be working at their full potential.	Keep in mind that writing quality is not determined by writing conventions. Address how well children are communicating their ideas as well as how well you can read what they write. You may find and acknowledge some beautiful sentiments in writing that is barely readable.
	• Students who struggle seem unengaged.	Acquaint yourself with the range of students' facility with conventions early on. Make sure your expectations for each child are reasonable. A child writing with mostly random letters will not benefit from being expected to use correct spelling and punctuation. Make sure you have mentor texts appropriate for all the ability levels in your class. Try conferring with struggling children a few extra times; they may need more individualized teaching until they have a better idea of what they can expect from themselves.

PROBLEM	WHAT IT LOOKS LIKE	POSSIBLE SOLUTION/ CONFERENCE
A sense of community has not yet developed.	• Children make comments that make other children feel bad ("That's easy! Anyone can do that!" or "He's bad, he always does stuff like that," or "That's wrong").	Community takes time to develop among children. Sometimes children make comments like these in an effort to be helpful to adults or to show that they are good. Model other ways to be helpful and other kinds of comments.
	• Children do not like their peers to have similar ideas ("You copied me!" or "She stole my idea!").	Why does this bother children so much?! Tell them that good ideas occur to people more often than bad ones, so it is natural to have plenty of ideas in common.
	• Children laugh aloud or sneer at peers' work.	Unlike the earlier comments, these seem intentionally hurtful. Be clear that such behavior is unacceptable and has consequences. Wanting to hurt others usually comes from hurting or feeling inadequate. Address these feelings with compassion at a time when the child is not being hurtful.

■ Assessment

To assess students at the end of a unit, you must revisit your goals. It is especially important to remember that there are not really any high, middle, or low writers. Rather, there are children with strengths and needs in different areas. A child with a strong sense of community may have difficulty getting to work without some reminders, and a great storyteller may have a lot to learn about commenting on the work of her peers. The rubric in Figure 1.2 is designed to help determine the needs of individual children and how to best address those needs in conferences and minilessons.

Though you have not yet begun to address writing conventions as a goal, you will soon. It will help to look now at what children are doing in this area so that you will have a better idea of how to determine the goals for the next unit of study. Lucy Calkins taught me a valuable assessment technique that really helps me focus on the children in my class and what they need to be taught. I sort the children's work into three or four piles and then look for patterns within each pile. The key here is that I do not try to sort the work into piles labeled *high*, *middle*, and *low*. Rather, I sort the work first and label later. As I am sorting, I look at different criteria, such as willingness to take risks by trying to spell unknown words, knowledge of letter–sound relationships, or comfort with spacing. This

BUILDING COMMUNITY	1 RARELY	2 SOMETIMES	3 MOST OF THE TIME	4 MORE THAN I EXPECT
Child listens and responds thoughtfully to the work of all other children.	☐	☐	☐	☐
Child shares own work.	☐	☐	☐	☐
Child enjoys hearing books read aloud and discusses books with classmates.	☐	☐	☐	☐
Child shares stories from his or her own life.	☐	☐	☐	☐
Child participates in shared retellings of class experiences.	☐	☐	☐	☐
WRITING HABITS				
Child participates in and follows up on some minilessons and conferences.	☐	☐	☐	☐
Child tries what is taught in minilessons and extends it to other pieces of writing.	☐	☐	☐	☐
Child moves and works quietly in the classroom.	☐	☐	☐	☐
Child has strategies to keep at work.	☐	☐	☐	☐
Child works independently.	☐	☐	☐	☐
Child treats tools and supplies with care.	☐	☐	☐	☐
Child sees writing possibilities everywhere (even at recess!).	☐	☐	☐	☐
WRITING QUALITY				
Child chooses topics that matter deeply.	☐	☐	☐	☐
Child tries a variety of genres or forms.	☐	☐	☐	☐
Child thinks of herself or himself as a writer with a message or story to tell.	☐	☐	☐	☐
Child's writing makes sense.	☐	☐	☐	☐
Most writing is focused on one topic.	☐	☐	☐	☐
WRITING CONVENTIONS				
Child writes with pictures and words.	☐	☐	☐	☐
Child writes left to right, top to bottom.	☐	☐	☐	☐
Child represents some sounds with the correct letters.	☐	☐	☐	☐

Figure 1.2 *Building Community Assessment Rubric*

helps me focus not on broad, perhaps preconceived, notions of what my students can and cannot do, but instead on what they need to meet my goals in this unit.

September writing could be sorted into the following three piles:

- *Children who are writing for the first time.* They make representative or nonrepresentative pictures, which may or may not include an attempt at writing words. They may tell oral stories to accompany these pictures. Children in this group may show great enthusiasm for writing or deep resistance and fear. Either way, you need to give them positive feedback and gentle encouragement to keep putting their stories and ideas into writing.

- *Children who have an idea of what writing is and are willing to put their stories and thoughts onto paper.* They are learning about the alphabet and how letters represent sounds as well as how they work together to make whole words. Their work consists of pictures and words, which may be random letters and/or symbols or may be readable though not conventionally spelled. Continue to encourage these children to write their ideas over several (at least three) pages and to reread their work often.

- *Children who feel comfortable writing their words first, without drawing a picture, but may have used one anyway.* Most of their words are conventionally spelled or close to it. They may have written a lot of words but have not necessarily developed the habits of planning before writing or reading and rereading after they write. Work with these children to develop these habits while encouraging continued progress.

Perhaps the most important thing to look for at the end of the first month of school is attitude. Watch children carefully as they work and listen to them as they talk about writing. Do they seem to have enthusiasm for writing? Do they plan projects? Do they refer to themselves as writers? Do they keep busy during writing workshop? Do they speak respectfully and thoughtfully about one another's work? They need to be personally invested in their own growth and development as writers. If you sense fear, lack of confidence, or resistance, address it immediately. Compliments are a good place to start. Compliments have an almost miraculous effect on the willingness of young writers to take risks and keep on trying things that take work to accomplish.

If all of these things are in place, and your classroom seems to hum with productivity and enthusiasm and you feel slightly out of control, your writing workshop is in perfect shape!

2 | Pattern Books

attern book is not a technical or literary term, but it's a helpful way to talk about the earliest books that children read conventionally. (By conventional reading, I mean reading and understanding the print, as opposed to the approximated reading that children do with fairy tales, folktales, and similar stories.) A pattern book has a predictable structure and repetitive language. Pattern books span a wide range of reading levels and may vary in how they adhere to or break away from a pattern. Most pattern books work like lists rather than stories. It makes sense to teach this unit early in the year because most first graders are reading books that contain patterns and because we want to begin our work on planning and organizing ideas with a simple text structure, one that is accessible to the full range of students.

■ Overview

This pattern book unit is about four weeks long, or twenty lessons. In the first few lessons, children are introduced to the idea of reading like writers, which Katie Wood Ray describes in beautiful detail in her book *Wondrous Words*. After that, children write their own pattern books, trying out some of the things they noticed in the published texts they read in the first few lessons. When they have finished at least one simple pattern book, children are ready to investigate more complex structures within the form. Throughout the unit, they learn to consider their readers by maintaining a consistent structure and topic. In preparation for publication, the teacher introduces them to new revision and editing techniques. When the unit is finished and the children have celebrated their work, the teacher encourages them to reflect on what they have learned.

▨ Goals

You must set reasonable goals for yourself and for your students based on what you observed in the last unit. The overall goals for the year have to do with writing quality, writing habits, community, and writing conventions. Knowing what you want children to be able to do by the end of the year, you can use your prior assessments to help you determine what you can expect by the end of *this month*.

One of the main qualities addressed in this unit is focus. You want students to be able to write whole pieces on one topic, pieces in which all the pages belong together. Working with a simple structure helps children achieve focus, which will help them later as they work with more complex structures. Also continue to work on habits of independence in spelling, choosing topics, and getting to work. When these are in place, children are able to develop more grown-up habits, such as learning from mentor authors or writing about a topic in a number of different genres. Your community is still pretty new, so your goals here may still have to do with keeping a respectful writing environment. You can also begin to teach children how writers discuss their work with one another.

Your goals for writing conventions should correspond to what you know about writing development in young children. If your students are using random strings of letters, you cannot yet expect them to use the spelling patterns of words they know on sight (like *make*) to help them spell new words (like *cake*). Rather, your goal should be for them to represent words with the beginning and ending sounds and sometimes the middle sounds. The following goals are based on my best guess of what most first graders need this month, but your students' needs may be different.

Writing Quality

Children will:

- Focus all the pages of one piece of writing on a single topic.

- Make conscious decisions about text structure.

- Use a simple text structure consistently through a whole piece of writing.

Writing Habits

Children will:

- Begin each workshop by looking over what is in their folders.

- Choose sometimes to begin a new piece of writing and sometimes to re-visit a piece of writing started on a previous day.

- Choose topics that they know and care a great deal about.

- Read and reread everything they write.

- Revise their work, with support and encouragement.

- Name simple writing moves and try them in their own writing. (For some children, this may mean matching the words to the picture, writing from left to right, or making the text follow a pattern. Other children may write vignettes, chapters of a nonfiction book, or steps in a process.)

Community

Children will:

- Be aware of which topics many of their peers have chosen.

- Offer help to classmates who need it.

- Share books with classmates.

- Share observations about books with classmates.

- Ask questions about and compliment classmates' work.

Writing Conventions

Children will:

- Put spaces between their words. (Some may still use dashes.)

- Represent most consonant sounds with the correct letter or letters.

- Spell correctly any words that are on the word wall.

With these goals in mind, it is appropriate to expect two published pattern books in four weeks—a simple one and a more challenging one. Some children will write many more than that while others will struggle to produce just two. The emphasis in writing the second book should be on challenging themselves; how they do this will be based on individual preference and readiness.

▨ Getting Ready to Teach

Writing workshop is most effective when we respond to and incorporate what children bring to it rather than adhere stringently to our plans. We give our students the best of our teaching and provide them with materials and a community of writers, and every now and then they clue us in to some great lessons we haven't thought of. The true purpose for lots of preparation, then, is to be able to use children's idiosyncrasies productively, not to avoid them. The better we gather and study our materials and the better we anticipate our children's needs, the better we can use whatever happens in the classroom to help our students continue to grow.

Considering the Students

First graders exhibit a wide spectrum of ability levels and attitudes toward writing. Looking at the first unit's assessment notes, you'll probably notice that many children rank differently in different areas of your rubric. One child might have a terrific sense of community but struggle to come up with ideas for writing; another might write with tight focus but have trouble getting started. All your students will benefit from all your lessons, but you need to adjust to their individual needs.

The needs of children who have difficulty developing a sense of community are the most difficult to address, since their inclination is to alienate themselves from others, including their teachers. Children who disrupt the community often do so because they don't feel part of the group and want to damage it. Excluding them further only confirms their feelings and makes the problem worse. You need to help them feel valued and loved. When possible, build their confidence in their own academic and social abilities. Validate all their positive interactions. Have individual conferences about how to respond to other children in the class and how to support the community. Some possible conference topics include the following:

- Saying "That's so easy" can hurt the feelings of children for whom something is not easy.

- When something is easy for you and difficult for a classmate, you can help her learn to do it better.

- Help classmates by reminding them of drawing, writing, or spelling strategies; don't do the work for them.

- One way to listen to a classmate's writing is to listen for things you like so that you can give him a compliment.

- When you share your work with other students, they get to know you better.

- When something is frustrating or hard for you, it is a good idea to ask for help.

Children who are having trouble developing good writing habits probably need help building their stamina for working. This will happen slowly and incrementally. Catching them in the act of working productively and complimenting them can keep them going for a few extra minutes. You also need to teach children a variety of ways to work during writing workshop: There are other ways to use this time besides writing. In individual conferences, remind children of the following:

- When you leave the meeting area, go right to your writing spot, open your folder, and read the last thing you were working on.

- Sometimes it's a good idea to look back through everything that's in your folder. You might find something you want to work on.

- If someone wants to talk to you and you are working, gently tell him to wait until later.

- The teacher's job in a conference is to teach something. Your job in a conference is to try what has been taught.

- The word wall offers some of the best spelling help in the classroom.

- Making a list of four or five things you know and care about most in this world will help you have topics when you need them.

Writing-quality goals in the previous unit centered mostly on how closely children identify with their writing. In other words, you want children to be writing things that really matter to them and writing in such a way that readers can understand the message. Children who have not yet quite gotten the hang of this will need your support in planning what they put on their papers and checking to make sure their work is clear and accurately conveys their thoughts. Here are some possible conference topics:

- Your work makes more sense if you plan what you will write before you start writing.

- Remember to reread after every sentence to make sure that your words say what you want them to.

- You can tell when a topic is a good one because it makes you feel excited to write about it. If you're not excited about your topic, you should probably pick a new one.

Finally, what you noticed when you looked at children's use of conventions at the end of the last unit will determine what you need to teach to individuals or small groups. You will probably teach most of these things, such as letter–sound relationships or how to spell frequently used words, outside of writing workshop. Here are some specific suggestions you can make:

- If you remember learning a word in word study, you can find it on the word wall.

- The ABC chart or the alphabet tape on your desk can help you decide which letter to write.

- After each word, you need to move your pen over a little before writing the next word, just as you move your finger over when you are reading.

- People can read your work more easily if you try to put important information into the picture.

During writing workshop you can help children use this knowledge in their own writing.

Gathering Books

We must love the texts we choose as mentors for our students. Our teaching becomes infused with this tenderness we have for literature, and our children adopt some of it themselves. That said, it can be hard to look with love and admiration at a text like "I like to play. I like to jump. I like to run." Nevertheless, I am acquainted with about a thousand such books, and there really are some I love—*Our Granny*, by Joy Cowley, for one. I can use it to help me teach some concepts with enthusiasm.

Before I teach this unit, I gather about thirty different pattern books from wherever I can: the classroom library, the school or local library, the school's book room, the book club bonus points I've been saving for a rainy day. I know I may not use all of these books, but I make sure to include a wide selection of topics and reading levels. My definition of a pattern book is pretty loose; I don't want to sift out anything that might be useful. The most important factor is loving the books—or at least liking them a lot.

As I read the books, I think about how they can become mentor texts in both minilessons and conferences. I ask myself what simple concepts a book can help me teach: labeling, writing left to right, word spacing. I notice specific ways in which it uses patterns: side-by-side lists, a repeated refrain, questions and answers. I also note how the pages of a pattern book work together to build a bigger idea: Are they parts of a whole? Kinds of a thing? Qualities of a thing? Steps in a process? I remember how a book uses beautiful or specific language. I write my ideas on sticky notes on the back covers and put the books in a basket on my desk. When I need an example of some technique an author uses, the books are right there, ready to help me teach.

Some possible mentor texts for this unit are listed in Appendix A.

Making Paper

It's also important to design paper that will support your objectives. Early in the study children sometimes have trouble writing several pages on one topic. Because it takes them a relatively long time to write just a few words, they can forget what they are writing about before they finish. The first paper I give my students has four boxes, each of which becomes a separate page when the writing is finished. There is little room for words, which helps children write a number of pages in a short time while keeping a handle on the overall structure of the book. Then, gradually, I introduce paper with only two boxes and more room for words. When I am confident that a child understands the text structure, I encourage him to use a single piece of paper for each page of the book.

I make all of these papers available at all times so children can explore them independently. (Reproducible examples of these paper formats are included in Appendix B.)

■ Teaching

Though the specific lessons you teach will vary from year to year, they should follow this general sequence: reading like writers, writing with intention,

TIME (A GENERAL GUIDELINE)	SECTION OF STUDY	WHAT NEEDS TO BE DONE IN THIS SECTION? *CHILDREN WILL:*
2–4 days	Reading Like Writers	• Get to know several pattern books. • Identify some individual structures within the form. • Notice decisions writers make in their work, such as topic, structure, word choice, and voice. • Think about the effects those decisions have on readers. • Start entering this information into the first four columns of the writing decisions chart.
5–7 days	Writing with Intention	• Choose and try some of the structures of pattern books that have been charted so far. • Be able to say what writing decisions they are making. • Keep patterns and topics consistent throughout their books. • Begin to think about how to match particular structures to their purposes as writers. • Fill in the "Have Any of Us Tried This?" column of the writing decisions chart and add more challenging texts in the first four columns.
7–8 days	Meeting a Bigger Challenge	• Challenge themselves by trying new or more complicated structures from the writing decisions chart (parallel lists, questions and answers, counting or growing sentences, cumulative sentences, refrains, etc.). • Challenge themselves by adding more text. • Add to the writing decisions chart, especially the "Have Any of Us Tried This?" column.
3–4 days	Revising and Editing	• Choose two pieces to publish. Repeat earlier editing technique and learn new one. • Learn new revision strategy. • Complete self-assessment questionnaire. • Celebrate!

Figure 2.1 *Pattern Books at a Glance*

meeting a bigger challenge, revising and editing, and publishing. (Writing with intention is making sure that what is written on the paper matches the idea the writer intends to communicate. This concept is also discussed briefly in the introduction.) Drafting a general calendar for the unit (see Figure 2.1) will help you stay on track and reach your ultimate goals.

Reading Like Writers

The first section of this study focuses on reading like writers, a brand-new concept for many children. You will already be a budding community of writers, speaking of yourselves as people who write. You will have read several pattern books to the children the week before and talked with them about some features of this structure. You will now be ready to start walking in writers' shoes, seeing with writers' eyes, hearing with writers' ears.

Reading like writers is an abstract concept. As with any other skill, you need to break it down for your students, teaching them the steps along the way. The goal here is that children *begin* to read like writers. So what part of reading like writers comes at the beginning? What part of the work do you do for them and what part can you expect them to do? One strong way to begin reading like a writer is immersing yourself in the kind of text that you can most easily envision yourself writing.

I spend the first three days of the study reading aloud a lot of pattern books and talking about them, jotting the children's thoughts next to mine on the sticky notes. Supporting students when they need it and backing off in order to encourage independence, I ask them what they notice authors doing in these pattern books and why they might be doing them. I record their thinking on a large classroom chart (see Figure 2.2), which we will refer to and add to during the rest of the study. The headings of the chart reflect the central questions of our inquiry:

What Do We Notice This Writer Doing?

Why? What Effect Does It Have on Us as Readers?

Name It.

Have Any of Us Tried This?

(Katie Wood Ray explores the thinking behind this chart in depth in *Wondrous Words*.)

Possible Teaching Points

- *Pattern books can have different structures. This is one kind of writing decision.* You want children to notice and distinguish between the different ways in which pattern books can be structured. After you have read and understood a book together, look at how the author organized her or his ideas. I demonstrate this first in a relatively simple book, such as *A Party*, by Joy

TITLE AND AUTHOR	WHAT DO WE NOTICE THIS WRITER DOING? (WRITING DECISIONS)	WHY? WHAT EFFECT DOES IT HAVE ON US AS READERS?	NAME IT	HAVE ANY OF US TRIED THIS?
A Party, by Joy Cowley	She names the thing that is in the picture.	It keeps the book simple. She tells us the name of the thing in the picture.	Labeling	
Water Changes, by Brenda Parkes	She tells us a bunch of information and then ends with a question.	She leaves us with something to think about.	Listing, with a question	
Baby Animals at Home, by Miriam Frost	She presents a question and an answer for each animal.	She doesn't just want to tell us something; she wants us to think before she tells us.	Presenting questions and answers	
Well Done, Worm! by Kathy Caple	She uses a pattern to tell a sequence of events.	It feels more like a story than a list.	Telling a story	
Our Granny, by Joy Cowley	She uses rhyming words to create a rhythm.	It sounds kind of like a song or a chant when we read it.	Rhyming	
When I Was Little, by Jamie Lee Curtis	She goes back and forth between when she was little and now.	On every page we can see how she is more grown up now than she was when she was a baby.	Going back and forth (seesawing)	
When I Was Five, by Arthur Howard	He makes two lists. Everything is different except one thing: his best friend.	We can see the difference between being five and being six, and we can see what's the same!	Making two lists	
This Train, by Paul Collicutt	He uses opposites to show different kinds of trains.	We can learn about many kinds of trains.	Giving opposites	

Figure 2.2 *Pattern Book Writing Decisions*

Cowley, and again in a more complex book, such as *When I Was Little,* by Jamie Lee Curtis. I might say, "I've read aloud *When I Was Little* a few times, and we understand this book pretty well. We've talked about it together a few times. This time when I read it, I am going to look at how Jamie Lee Curtis decided to put this book together. Let's see . . . she seems to use the words *when I was little* and *now* on every page. She goes back and forth between these two ways of starting a sentence. It turns into a sort of list of things that changed."

- *Writers study the work of other writers, thinking about why they might have made certain decisions in their writing.* Extend the prior lesson by teaching children how to look at the effects certain writing decisions have on us as readers. This concept sounds fancier than it is, so children will need to see a demonstration. I show them a familiar book like *When I Was Little* and remind them how the pattern works, going back and forth between the past and the present. Then I show them clearly how this decision affects the reader: "The way the author uses this pattern really shows us how much more grown up she is now than she was when she was little."

- *Writing decisions include more than just the topic.* Topic is one important choice a writer has to make, but there are others. Children's ideas of a writing decision often have only to do with the topic. Teach your students about the other kinds of decisions authors make in their books, such as word choice, sentence length; sentence structure; text structure; interesting punctuation; use of dialogue, voice, and genre.

- *Even simple pattern books are the result of writing decisions.* Many children are just beginning to understand the concept of reading, never mind reading like writers. Show them how to make their own pattern books like the ones they are reading independently. You might say, "I know you were reading *A Party* in reading workshop today. I have a feeling *you* could write a book like that. Instead of a party, it could be about something *you* really care about, like painting or playing dress-up. What do you think? May I teach you how to get started on that?"

- *More difficult pattern books are the result of more sophisticated writing decisions.* A child may be able to read a more difficult book, like *When I Was Young in the Mountains,* by Cynthia Rylant, this early in the year. However, learning how a language pattern can link a series of vignettes may require some coaching: "I think she starts each page the same way for a reason. It begins to sound like a song to me. It also connects all these little stories for me, so I know that they all have to do with one another. What does it do for you when *you* read these repeated words?"

Writing with Intention

After a few days of reading books and discussing them as writers, it's time to move on to the second section of the study. In these five or six lessons, children start to write their own pattern books. These lessons focus on intention: thinking about what you are going to write before you get to work, imagining how you are going to write, rereading your work, and considering your readers—in other words, making your own writing decisions. Because the particular kind of writing decision you want to emphasize is that of structure, you should expect the children to be able to name the structure they are going to try in their writing and to say why they are trying it.

Continue to add to the writing decisions chart, especially the "Have Any of Us Tried This?" column (see Figure 2.3). As children explore different writing decisions in their books, copy their work and tape it to the chart. This makes the chart an even more useful reference. Students can now see not only how published writers work but also how writers in their own class make decisions in their writing. They need time to explore using text structure differently in pattern books, and they need the freedom to take risks—to try things that may not work out. Encourage them to try new structures rather than become comfortable in a routine type of writing. Most children will write a few books this week and will have at least *tried* several of the structures they identified in the first few days of the study.

Possible Teaching Points

- ***One pattern writers use to create books is labeling.*** Some pattern books have only one or two words on each page, words that name the item depicted in the illustration. Teach children how to make a pattern book that works the same way. On a chart divided to look like four-box paper, draw four things that go together (and about which the students know and care a great deal). Then go back and add the words. Children learn not only to make this kind of book but also, by extension, that they can make books like *any* of the books in their classroom.

- ***Authors also use the back-and-forth pattern to create books.*** This kind of book is like two pattern books on related topics that have been shuffled together. The pages go back and forth between the topics, describing how they are similar or different. A book about butterflies and moths, for example, could be a back-and-forth book. Show children how to make a book like this, pointing out that the topics are similar and different at the same time. Choose a familiar topic to help make this clear: "I'm going to show you how Jackie's book about butterflies and moths is a back-and-forth book. You see, these insects are similar, but they are also different. Let me show you her book. 'A butterfly starts as a caterpillar. A moth starts as a caterpillar. A butterfly makes a chrysalis. A moth makes a cocoon.' See? She uses the pattern to tell us how butterflies and moths are similar and different."

- ***Writers create books using many kinds of patterns.*** Any pattern that a writer uses in a book can be the subject of a minilesson like the previous ones. The important thing is to demonstrate, clearly and simply, how to make that kind of book.

TITLE AND AUTHOR	WHAT DO WE NOTICE THIS WRITER DOING? (WRITING DECISIONS)	WHY? WHAT EFFECT DOES IT HAVE ON US AS READERS?	NAME IT	HAVE ANY OF US TRIED THIS?
A Party, by Joy Cowley	She names the thing that is in the picture.	It keeps the book simple. She tells us the name of the thing in the picture.	Labeling	Dasha labeled her favorite toys in her book.
Water Changes, by Brenda Parkes	She tells us a bunch of information and then ends with a question.	She leaves us with something to think about.	Listing, with a question	Jackie's book makes you think at the end.
Baby Animals at Home, by Miriam Frost	She has a question and an answer for each animal.	She doesn't just want to tell us something; she wants us to think before she tells us.	Presenting questions and answers	Alexis did this in her book *What Is in the Flowers?*
Well Done, Worm! by Kathy Caple	She uses a pattern to tell a sequence of events.	It feels more like a story than a list.	Telling a story	
Our Granny, by Joy Cowley	She uses rhyming words to create a rhythm.	It sounds kind of like a song or a chant when we read it.	Rhyming	
When I Was Little, by Jamie Lee Curtis	She goes back and forth between when she was little and now.	On every page we can see how she is more grown up now than she was when she was a baby.	Going back and forth (seesawing)	Jackie did this in her book about butterflies and moths.
When I Was Five, by Arthur Howard	He makes two lists. Everything is different except one thing: his best friend.	We can see the difference between being five and being six, and we can see what's the same!	Making two lists	
This Train, by Paul Collicutt	He uses opposites to show different kinds of trains.	We can learn about many kinds of trains.	Giving opposites	Owen wrote about food that is good and food that isn't good.
When I Was Young in the Mountains, by Cynthia Rylant	She begins each page with the same words and then describes a little scene from her life.	The pattern helps us see how all the scenes go together.	Linking scenes (vignettes)	Owen and Sarah both wrote books that do this!
Hairs/Pelitos, by Sandra Cisneros	She goes back and forth between the two languages she speaks, English and Spanish. There is a pattern, but it changes a little.	Maybe she wants us to know that her family is from two places at the same time.		Klara wrote her book in English and Polish.
Birthday Presents, by Cynthia Rylant	She counts the years in which she received various birthday presents. She writes a lot.	We get to watch her grow up.	Counting the years	Rebecca wrote a book that shows how she has grown up over time.

Figure 2.3 *Updated Chart of Pattern Book Writing Decisions*

- *Writers use a consistent pattern throughout a whole book.* When coming back to a piece of writing started on a previous day, it's important for children to read what they've already written before continuing to write so that the pattern will be consistent. If a child wants to change a pattern, she should change it throughout the whole book, not just on the last pages. Demonstrate this with a piece of writing you have created ahead of time that does not stay on one topic or is not finished. Show how you stop and ask yourself, "How is my pattern working? If I add more pages, what do I need to do to make sure it keeps working the same way? If some pages don't match, I can either change them or just take them out and make a whole new book out of them."

- *Writers choose a pattern that matches their purpose.* Some ideas lend themselves to certain kinds of patterns. A book about butterflies and moths could use opposite words to highlight the differences between the two insects, or it could contain side-by-side lists to show similarities and differences. A book about favorite toys or candy might use the same sentence structure throughout but have a surprise ending, thus giving one thing special status above a group of similar things. Demonstrate how you might decide to use a particular pattern to help get a point across more clearly: "Well, I like Skittles and Necco wafers and Redhots, but I absolutely love Hot Tamales! I could use a pattern that is the same for all the candy I like and then change it to show how special Hot Tamales are."

- *Writers keep the whole book on one topic.* Some children will need support in staying on one topic. For example, a child's book might say, "I play soccer. I play jacks. I play bingo. My friend Joe-Joe is fun." If a new and captivating topic enters a child's mind as he is writing about another one, he should explore it *in a new piece of writing* rather than try to finish the old piece with the new topic in mind. Teach your students that it can be a good idea to start a new piece of writing without finishing the current one: "Well, this pattern book is about animals I like, but now I want to write about the games I play on the weekend. I could just add that on to this book, but that wouldn't really make sense. I'm going to save this animal book for later and start a whole new book about the games."

- *Writers make sure the pages go together.* Even after teaching the previous lesson, you may still notice that a child has a book in which some of the pages do not seem to belong. Make a similar book to use as a demonstration tool and say, "Watch how I look through my book to see if the pages go together.

This page has my mom, and this page has my dad. OK, those two go together; let's see what's next. My *pencil?!?* That does not go with my mom and my dad! My mom and my dad are people in my family, and my pencil is one of my tools for writing workshop. I need to take that page away and add a few more pages that go with my mom and my dad. Maybe other people in my family?" Trying the same thing in her own book will be less scary for a child if she has already seen you do it and knows it is not such a big deal.

- *If writers can't read their writing or if it doesn't make sense, they stop and fix the problem.* There are a number of reasons writing can be hard to read, and a single lesson can cover all of them: penmanship, spelling, using words that get in the way of understanding the message. Leave it up to children to decide whether their writing makes sense and looks right and to fix it if it does not. Show them how you read your words for meaning, sense, spelling, and neatness (not that their writing has to be perfectly neat, but the letters have to be formed well enough that someone can tell what they are). I tell them, "When you see problems, don't beat yourself up but simply fix the issue and move on."

Meeting a Bigger Challenge

This section of the study digs deeper into the idea of writing with intention, emphasizing trying new ideas and meeting a challenge. Children start to write more text, trying different structures for their pattern books or adding more information to each page. This is a time of intense work, but don't push children to do different work every day. You simply want students to work on one piece of writing over several days. Meeting a challenge is going to mean different things to different children. I use writing samples from the class to help me illustrate possible challenges. Again, post this work in the "Have Any of Us Tried This?" section of the chart.

Possible Teaching Points

- *One way to meet a bigger challenge is to write more words on each page.* Some children will now be writing book after book, with some folders containing twenty books! Congratulate children on their productivity and gently steer them toward writing fewer books with greater detail or elaboration. A good way to demonstrate this is to prepare a fairly simple pattern book and show the class how you can add information to it. A book could go from "I like apples. I like oranges" to "I like apples. There are lots of kinds of apples, but my favorite is Gala. Apples have seeds, and if you cut them in half a certain way, the seeds make a star."

- *Another way to meet a challenge is to write about a more complicated idea.* You will need to teach some children how to use more sophisticated structures to help communicate their ideas. Knowing a variety of books well will come in handy. Guide children to books that match their ideas. For example, Klara wanted to write about her family in both Polish and English. Instead of writing everything there is to know about the members of her family, she wanted to include one thing they all have in common (being Polish) and one thing that is different about them all. She was able to get inspiration from *Hairs/Pelitos,* by Sandra Cisneros (see Figure 2.4). Rebecca wanted to write about her birthday parties as a window into how she has grown up a little more each year of her life. She found help in *Birthday Presents,* by Cynthia Rylant (see Figure 2.5). Other possible mentor texts for writing about a more complicated idea are listed in Appendix A.

- *Writers have things they do when they think they are done.* Even though you've already taught a minilesson about this, some children will still need help. A classroom chart of things to do when you think you are done is a good place to start. Have conferences on this topic as necessary, perhaps making an individual checklist of things to do when a particular child says she's done. You can also give individual advice: "Take a walk around the classroom without disturbing any other writers and then sit down and get to work," or "Look at one book from the class library for five minutes and then get back to work." You may not be able to force children to build stamina, but you can make sure that when they run out of it, they do not bother anyone. This will help them for years to come!

- *Writers use what they know to help them spell what they don't know.* Children who ask you how to spell certain words may be ready and able to transfer spelling skills. I say, "If you know how to spell *and,* then you also know how to spell *hand,* and you have a pretty good idea how to spell *candy* or *panda.*" When you help children gain independence as spellers, you can use more of your time teaching them to be better *writers.*

Revising and Editing

The final section of the study is a short one. It involves getting ready for the final celebration and should take about three days. Children choose two pieces to publish, one from the first round of writing and one from the second. In the

My hair is blond and a little tiny bit curly.

My hair is blond and a little tiny bit curly.

My dad has hair a little bit up.

My dad has hair a little bit up.

Figure 2.4 Hair/Wtosy, *by Klara*

On my third birthday we played pass the package.

On my fourth birthday my birthday cake was Barbie.

Figure 2.5 My Birthdays, *by Rebecca*

prior unit, you introduced a revision strategies chart and an editing checklist. So far, each has only one item on it. In this study (and all the rest), you will add another item to each and ask students do some basic editing and polishing of their work.

Possible Teaching Points

- *Writers take away pages or words that do not seem to belong.* In the last unit, you taught children how to add to their ideas. This month, teach the complementary strategy of taking away pages, sentences, or words that do not help their pieces. Refer back to the lessons about keeping the whole book on one topic. Encourage children to remove pages from their books that do not seem to belong. Also, ask them to make sure they do not have extra words, perhaps ones that are left over from a previous revision. The key strategy here is to get them to reread their work, asking, "Does this go with the rest of my book?" after every page.

- *One way to begin or end a pattern book is by saying what the whole book is about.* In introducing pattern books, you probably synthesized information, saying what the whole book was about, not just restating what was written on some of the pages. Some children may be ready to try this with their writing as well. Demonstrate this with a pattern book that you have prepared in advance. For example, I show a book I have made that says, "Our classroom has a block center. We like to build things in there. Sometimes people work on a building for a whole week. Our classroom has a science observation center. The teacher puts out different kinds of things from nature for us to look at and sketch. We have a microscope and magnifying glasses so we can see things close up." There are a few more similar pages. Then I show how I can make a new page for the beginning or end of this book that encompasses the whole thing: "Our classroom has lots of centers. They are fun and they also help us learn."

- *Writers make sure their sentences end with periods and begin with capital letters.* Remember that the skill is not so much putting periods and capitals in the right places as it is understanding what a sentence is! It doesn't make sense to get into subjects and predicates with primary writers. Instead, rely on intuition. Prepare a demonstration text by writing a few sentences that look and sound pretty much like those your students write but *without periods or capitals.* Then show children how you read your writing to yourself slowly, listening for the times your voice wants to stop. "Usually, my voice wants to stop at the ends of sentences. 'My friend Julia has a really big lawn mower.' I heard my voice stop right then; did you hear it? Let me make sure that's a whole idea. 'My friend Julia has a really big lawn mower.' Yep! That's a whole idea, so I will put a period there. If it just ended at *has* or *big,* that wouldn't be the whole idea. Of course, the very next letter after a period has to be capital, so I'll just do that right now."

- *Writers don't forget previous revision and/or editing strategies.* Though you have posted the revision and editing checklists from the first unit as charts in the classroom, not everyone will be using them. You will undoubtedly need to teach children to remember to use the strategies they have learned for editing and revision. Model this with the same piece of writing you used in prior editing and revision lessons. "I checked my capitals and periods yesterday. Today I'm going to look at my piece of writing and make sure there are spaces between all the words. I'm also going to see if I want to add more information."

Publishing

At the end of the unit, have a grand celebration to which you invite parents and friends. Your last celebration was small and intimate to help a fragile new community bond. This month your community is strong enough to invite loved ones to see what you have created together. Many parents work during the day, but they will make an effort to get to their children's writing celebrations if they can. In order to make it easier for them, I like to hold the events first thing in the morning. It's nice for children to be able to read their work aloud, but it takes a long time to hear the whole class, and most students don't read aloud well enough to engage the parents of *other* children. When parents started asking, "Can my kid go first? I really have to get to work [or the grocery store or the dog groomer]," I instituted museum celebrations in which students read their pieces aloud only to the children who share their table and their guests. This takes only about fifteen minutes, and both children and guests pay better attention. After that, they leave their writing at their tables and roam the room to look at other children's writing. Each table has a comment sheet for parents to fill out. Parents who have to leave can go without feeling as if they're sneaking out, and parents who wish to stay can see more work.

▪ Predictable Problems

When things go wrong, it does not mean we are not doing a good job. We just need to determine the cause of the problem and address it. Some issues that are common in this unit and possible ways to address them follow.

PROBLEM	WHAT IT LOOKS LIKE	POSSIBLE SOLUTION/ CONFERENCE
You have under-planned for the unit.	• You do not have any/enough mentor texts. • You do not know what you want students to be doing. • You have no ideas for minilessons. • Your minilessons seem unclear. • Your minilessons have too many teaching points.	Stop teaching writing for a day and give yourself time to regroup. Go over your lesson plans; look through children's writing folders; get some books to use as models, look through them, and choose a couple of simple things to teach. Allow yourself to teach a few consecutive minilessons on the same topic until you feel clearer about where to take the study next. Now you'll be able to make this clearer to the children.

PROBLEM	WHAT IT LOOKS LIKE	POSSIBLE SOLUTION/ CONFERENCE
You have over-planned for the unit.	• The children seem unable to do what you ask. • You cannot find a student whose work you wish to share. • It just is not going how you wanted it to.	Try to look at what your students *are* doing, rather than at what they are *not* doing. Plan the next few minilessons based on what you see them doing in their work. Spend a few days using children's writing as models for your minilessons so that the class can get a clearer sense of what you expect from them.
The class shows a lack of interest.	• Children are not working. • Children say, "I'm done!" during the workshop. • Children say, "Awww," when it is time for writing workshop.	Try writing a pattern book together as a whole class; then add the book to your classroom library. Allot a little extra time to share writing for a few days so that you can show the class several examples of student work. Try teaching one or two mini-lessons in which you fishbowl what good conferences look like. Make sure you are talking about writing as if you are the luckiest person in the world to get to teach it (which you are, by the way).
The class shows a lack of basic understanding.	• Children copy directly from mentor texts. • The pages in students' writing do not seem to go together. • Children's writing choices are related only to topic.	If the issue is limited to just a few students, you may want to pull them aside for a semiprivate minilesson or for a supported writing group. If the whole class is having a problem, you will need to simplify your minilessons, refer to simpler published mentor texts, and model some examples of pattern books that are within the children's range of ability.
You're not reaching all learners.	• More advanced students do not appear to be working at their full potential. • Struggling students have no idea what to do or how to do it.	Be sure you have mentor texts appropriate to the ability levels in your class. Try conferring with these children more often; they may need more individualized teaching until they have a better idea of what they can expect from themselves.

▣ Assessment

Your students' published pieces are one kind of assessment. They are how you really determine whether children are able to write a whole piece on one topic, a piece that follows a consistent structure and in which they purposefully try to write in ways they have seen in published pattern books. Finished pieces also tell you how children revise and edit their work and which writing conventions they are using consistently or are beginning to use.

I also like to have children complete some kind of self-assessment, such as filling out a questionnaire about their work (see Figure 2.6). I might ask them what they did well, what they found difficult, and what they would like to try again. Learning about their attitude toward writing and their opinion of their own work influences how I confer with individual students. The questionnaire also tells me what was clear in my teaching and what I may have to address again in future units. If ten students find it difficult to add information to work started on a previous day, for example, I probably need to find another way to demonstrate it.

More formal assessment involves revisiting your goals for your students and evaluating whether they are being met. Using rubrics (see Figure 2.7) helps you evaluate your own teaching, determine your children's needs and strengths, and set future goals.

Name _____ Date _____

WOW!! We are ready to celebrate our pattern books and all the hard work that went into them.

What did you do really well in your book?

_____

_____

_____

_____

What was difficult for you?

_____

_____

_____

_____

Tell me one new thing you learned this month.

_____

_____

_____

_____

Figure 2.6 *Self-Assessment Questionnaire for Pattern Books*

WRITING QUALITY	1 RARELY	2 SOMETIMES	3 MOST OF THE TIME	4 MORE THAN I EXPECT
Child focuses all the pages of one piece of writing on a single topic.	❏	❏	❏	❏
Child makes conscious decisions about text structure.	❏	❏	❏	❏
Child uses a simple text structure consistently through a whole piece of writing.	❏	❏	❏	❏

WRITING HABITS

	1 RARELY	2 SOMETIMES	3 MOST OF THE TIME	4 MORE THAN I EXPECT
Child begins each workshop by looking over what is in his/her folder.	❏	❏	❏	❏
Child chooses sometimes to begin a new piece of writing and sometimes to revisit a piece of writing started on a previous day.	❏	❏	❏	❏
Child chooses topics that she/he knows and cares a great deal about.	❏	❏	❏	❏
Child tries what is taught in minilessons and extends it to other pieces of writing.	❏	❏	❏	❏
Child reads and rereads everything he/she writes.	❏	❏	❏	❏
Child revises her/his work, with support and encouragement.	❏	❏	❏	❏
Child names simple writing moves and tries them in his/her own writing (for some children, this may mean matching the words to the picture, writing from left to right, or making the text follow a pattern; other children may write vignettes, chapters of a nonfiction book, or steps in a process).	❏	❏	❏	❏

COMMUNITY

	1 RARELY	2 SOMETIMES	3 MOST OF THE TIME	4 MORE THAN I EXPECT
Child is aware of which topics many of her/his peers have chosen.	❏	❏	❏	❏
Child offers help to classmates who need it.	❏	❏	❏	❏
Child shares books and observations about books with classmates.	❏	❏	❏	❏
Child asks questions about and compliments classmates' work.	❏	❏	❏	❏

WRITING CONVENTIONS

	1 RARELY	2 SOMETIMES	3 MOST OF THE TIME	4 MORE THAN I EXPECT
Child puts spaces between words (some may still use dashes).	❏	❏	❏	❏
Child represents most sounds with the correct letter or letters.	❏	❏	❏	❏
Child spells correctly any words that are on the word wall.	❏	❏	❏	❏

Figure 2.7 *Pattern Book Assessment Rubric*

3

Nonfiction Question-and-Answer Books

C hildren should study nonfiction writing several times during the year. Because adopting the authoritative voice necessary for nonfiction can be difficult, it's best for them to work in a structure in the fall that is only slightly more complicated than the one they have just studied. This unit raises the bar not by introducing a whole new text structure but by fostering independence and extending your students' knowledge and skill within a subcategory of pattern books: questions and answers. This early in the year, students' command of writing conventions, experience with text structures, knowledge of themselves as writers, and stamina for writing in a single sitting on a single topic are still rudimentary. It's best to keep the structure simple. (Later in the year, you can introduce richer, more complicated nonfiction. *Nonfiction Writing: Procedures and Reports,* by Lucy Calkins and Laurie Pessah, part of the Units of Study for Primary Writing series, is an excellent resource.)

Primary classes generally include students with a wide range of abilities. The writing you ask children to do should challenge all children, whether they are just beginning to write or are already fluent writers. In this unit, you will be able to stretch your more experienced students' minds if you include examples of question-and-answer books at more advanced reading levels. You should also be ready to let children break away from the structure completely if they seem ready.

A good nonfiction writing study should closely follow or coincide with a study of nonfiction reading. Much of what you want the children to come to understand about nonfiction can be learned more fully through reading *and* writing. It is a small and logical step from teaching that when a nonfiction book asks the reader a question, the reader's job is to be able to answer that question at the end of the book or section to teaching that if a nonfiction *writer* asks a question, his or her job is to answer that question for the reader. If you have a reading workshop ongoing in your classroom, *Growing Readers,* by Kathy Collins, is an excellent resource.

Also remember that the majority of children's time in writing workshop should be spent writing, not doing research. They'll need a separate time in which to confirm or gather facts.

■ Overview

This unit should take no longer than three weeks. (Presumably you'll be doing another nonfiction study later in the year, thus giving children an additional opportunity to explore this kind of writing and develop their nonfiction voice more fully.) Begin with an in-depth look at different types of question-and-answer books. Encourage students to notice variations within this form and to think about why an author might have chosen one of these variations over another. During the unit, each child should produce several books, finally choosing one or two to publish. The last few days are spent revising and editing the final published piece.

■ Goals

This is a great unit to get kids thinking more independently about writing books that contain enough but not too much information, because they are writing in a structure that most of them can easily understand. This will help them make their books seem complete. Because the question-and-answer format is similar to a list, children can easily decide how much information to include. They can also hone their ability to make consistent structure and content decisions.

Writing Quality

Children will:

- Write with an authoritative or knowledgeable voice. Their word choice and sentence structure will reflect their knowledge of their topic.

- Make conscious decisions about text structure.

- Keep structure and topic consistent through the whole book.

- Be able to name the topic of their book, give it an appropriate title, and describe the content of the whole book in a few words.

- Show that they understand the relationship between whole and part by telling how an individual page connects to the topic of the whole book.

Writing Habits

Children will:

- Choose topics that they know and care a great deal about and that are suitable for nonfiction.

- Reread everything they write.

- Revise their work, with support.

Writing Conventions

Children will:

- Put spaces between their words (one or two may still use dashes).

- Form letters correctly or fix improperly formed letters independently.

- Spell correctly any words that are on the word wall (words they have learned in spelling or word study).

Community

Children will:

- Be aware of which topics many of their peers have chosen.

- Be able to make some smart decisions about which peers to ask for help with different writing issues.

- Participate in conversations about books and writing.

■ Getting Ready to Teach

Keep in mind your assessment information from the prior unit of study so that your lessons will match children's needs. Also make sure you have the supplies your students will need in order to do the best work they can.

Considering the Students

The most important part of getting ready to teach the unit is weighing the strengths and needs of the children in the class. This is a good time to go back over your assessment notes from the pattern book unit and use this information to prepare possible lessons or individual conferences for this unit.

In the pattern book unit, the writing quality you were working to develop was consistency, of both topic and structure. Children who had trouble achieving this will need some additional support with making decisions about how their books will work and then sticking to those decisions. You may decide to echo some pattern book minilessons in individual conferences. For example:

● Remember to decide how your book will work before you start writing it.

● Make sure all of your pages are about the same thing.

● Read your book to make sure it works the way you wanted it to.

Some children may need continued support in order to internalize the habits you're teaching and become more independent as writers. Sometimes you need to remind children what you want them to do, but you also need other strategies to help them become more responsible and active in the writing workshop. Your conferences might focus on the following points:

● At the start of each workshop, remember to look in your folder at what you were working on before.

● You must both know and care a lot about your topic.

● Read your writing with questions in mind: Does it make sense? Is this what I meant to say? Are all the words there? Have I learned any of these words in word study or spelling?

● You can look at some published books for ideas about how to make your own book.

Your hope is that children who are having trouble being active in the classroom community are at least kind and respectful toward the other children. The pattern book unit's goals for establishing community emphasize how children work together. Continue that work this month in your conferences, teaching children how to ask for and accept help as well as how to give help in a way that really is helpful:

- Writers learn from other writers by reading their work or by just asking them for help. You can learn from all the writers in this classroom.

- Good writers know whom to ask for help, depending on what is difficult and what they know others are good at.

- In order to help other writers, you need to give them strategies they can use, not just tell them what to write.

Your goals for writing conventions should reflect what is appropriate for *most* children to learn. Not all students will master those conventions at the same rate. Be aware of which students need support with conventions and give it to them. Some writing conventions are taught outside the writing workshop—in shared or interactive writing, word study, or phonics, for example. In writing workshop, though, you must teach children how to use what they have learned in these other settings. Being prepared to address these needs will help you take them in stride when they arise. Points of focus include the following:

- Writing goes from left to right.

- The ABC chart helps you know which letters to write for beginning, ending, or middle sounds.

- Words need to have spaces between them.

- Work is easier to read if it stays on the lines.

Gathering Books

Fortunately, many elementary-level nonfiction books have some sort of question-and-answer format. Teachers I work with on this unit always manage to find enough books either in their own classrooms or somewhere in the school (a book room or other teachers' rooms). Ideally, you should have a stack of about twenty books spanning reading levels from late kindergarten through third grade and representing a number of variations on the question-and-answer format. Again, it is important to love or at least see lots of teaching possibilities in the books you will be using.

I read the books I have gathered with a pack of sticky notes by my side, jotting down things I might teach during the unit, either to the whole class or to individuals. I want to know how the books work and how I might use them to help me teach.

A list of possible books is included in Appendix A.

Making Paper

Two-box paper is so versatile that I use it all year. It gives children room to draw an illustration and write a few sentences about it and then turn to a new page and write about a new idea and draw a new illustration, thus keeping their writing to a single topic. However, it's time to get rid of the four-box paper. All children should now be expected to write more words and to hold on to an idea long enough to write a book across several sheets.

New paper prepared especially for this study should include separate lines for questions and answers. While most children will be able to decide independently where to place their ideas on the page, paper like this supports those who are feeling a little shaky about using this structure consistently across a whole book.

Finally, support the more fluent writers by providing paper with more lines and helping them write more about their ideas.

■ Teaching

In this unit of study children learn to write nonfiction books that, at least loosely, follow a question-and-answer pattern. Since they have used patterns in their writing in the previous unit, you can refer back to and build on those experiences. The main new learning in this unit relates to writing nonfiction, or informational, texts. As children are writing their books and making decisions about topic and structure, you need to prepare lessons and conferences that address some particular requirements of informational writing.

Children should choose topics about which they know and care a great deal. Nonfiction writers must know enough about their topics so they can teach others about them. Children should be able to tell you, in just a few words, what they are writing about. You want them to be able to talk both about the whole book and about each page within the book. As with their earlier general pattern books, it should be clear how all the pages work together. Finally, you want

TIME (A GENERAL GUIDELINE)	SECTION OF STUDY	WHAT NEEDS TO BE DONE IN THIS SECTION? *CHILDREN WILL:*
1 day (and ongoing)	Reading Like Writers	• Get to know several nonfiction question-and-answer books. • Identify some variations within the form. • Help fill in the writing decisions chart
4–6 days	Writing with Intention	• Choose appropriate topics. • Try some of the types of question-and-answer books they've examined so far. • Be able to say what they are trying. • Be able to say why. • Add to the writing decisions chart, thinking about why authors chose certain forms for their particular topics.
5–7 days	Meeting a Bigger Challenge	• Try a new or more challenging form. • Try adding more text. • Try a more complicated kind of book. • Fill in the column on the writing decisions chart identifying which students in the class have tried different kinds of books.
2–3 days	Revising and Editing	• Choose two pieces to publish. • Learn a new revision strategy (taking away things that do not belong) and add it to the checklist. • Learn a new editing strategy (fix backward letters) and add it to the checklist.
1–2 days	Publishing	• Complete self-assessment questionnaire. • Celebrate!

Figure 3.1 *Nonfiction at a Glance*

them to understand that nonfiction books are factual and provide information, not opinions or stories.

Before you can plan each lesson needed to teach these skills explicitly, you should draft a general map of your journey toward the intended outcomes (see Figure 3.1). Since the sections of this study are similar to those in the pattern book unit, children will find the progression familiar and comfortable.

Reading Like Writers

Like the pattern book unit, this one starts with looking at published books. Because the question-and-answer format is a subcategory of pattern books, you can devote one day to reading the books instead of three. As soon as the second day, children can be writing their own books. However, they should continue to read the published books, observing how they're set up, throughout the entire study. Raise the bar this month (and move closer to achieving the year's goals) by teaching children to look more closely at writers' reasons for making certain writing decisions. Encourage students to participate more actively in your

TITLE AND AUTHOR	WHAT DO WE NOTICE THIS WRITER DOING? (WRITING DECISIONS)	WHY? WHAT EFFECT DOES IT HAVE ON US AS READERS?	NAME IT	HAVE ANY OF US TRIED THIS?
What Does a Garden Need? by Judy Nayer *What Lays Eggs?* by Katherine Gracestozne *Who Beats the Heat?* by Pamela Chanko and Daniel Moreton	They give many answers to one question.	It helps us learn how different kinds of things are also sort of the same.	Question–answer– answer–answer	
Will We Miss Them? Endangered Species, by Alexandra Wright *What's Under the Log?* by Anne Hunter	They give long answers to their questions.	It tells us all about something, not just a little bit.	Question–a-n-s-w-e-r	
Baby Animals at Home, by Miriam Frost *What's Inside?* by Colin Walker	They ask different questions and answer each one.	It teaches us about different things that have something in common.	Question–answer– different question– different answer– different question– different answer	
Where Are the Seeds? by Pauline Cartwright *Seeds, Seeds, Seeds,* by Brian and Jillian Cutting	They ask the same question and give different answers.	It teaches us about different qualities of one thing.	Question–answer– same question– different answer– same question– different answer	
What's Inside? by Mary Jane Martin *Baby Animals at Home,* by Miriam Frost	They put the answers on the reverse side of the pages containing the questions.	It makes us think a little before we get to see the answer.	Question–think– answer	

Figure 3.2 *Nonfiction Question-and-Answer Book Writing Decisions*

conversations as you fill in the "Why?" column of the writing decisions chart (see Figure 3.2). Most children will be ready to take this step, with support.

What about the children who are not? Knowing your children a little better this month, you can put more thought into how to meet the needs of a wide range of writers. Continue to refer to a range of books that reflect varying reading levels, pattern complexities, and amounts of information. You want all children to be able to challenge themselves.

Possible Teaching Points

- *All of these books have questions and answers. Let's look at what makes them different.* Show children that even though all the books they are looking at have questions and answers, they exemplify many different ways of organizing information. Add these different formats to a new chart of writing decisions made especially for this unit. Ask why the authors may have chosen to put their books together the way they did.

- *How would this look if you tried it in your own writing?* As children look through the collection of mentor books, present a minilesson on how certain formats might work if they were to try them in their own writing, with their own ideas: "So in this book each question has three or four different answers. What if we wrote about our classroom that way? I guess if we asked, 'What can kids do at center time?' the answers could be 'Kids can paint with watercolors or tempera paints; kids can build things with blocks or Legos; kids can play games'; and so on."

Writing with Intention

Remind the class that writers not only have to know about their topic but also have to care about it. Often children write informational texts about topics that interest them but about which they have little knowledge, or vice versa. You also need to teach children to choose topics that are suitable for nonfiction writing. A child knows a lot about his mother, and he cares deeply for her, and he can write facts about her, but "my mother" isn't a very good nonfiction topic. He should save that topic for narrative writing.

Once again, emphasize the idea that writers create texts with a specific intention. Children know that since they are in school, they are going to have work to do. It's difficult to get them to write something because they *want* to. When you focus your lessons on the idea of having an intention or a purpose for writing, rather than on doing something right, you teach children that writing is primarily an act of communication with the world. In nonfiction, intention often translates into wanting to teach your readers, or audience, about something important to you. Sharing children's work is vital to building a strong intention for writing. It needs to be true when we tell them that their work has an audience.

A helpful strategy for getting children to be intentional about how they write their nonfiction books is to teach them to ask themselves what their readers absolutely *must* know about the topic: "If I want to teach people about our fish tank, my readers absolutely must know about the gravel in the bottom, the kinds of fish we have, the food, the light, and how to clean it out. What do your readers absolutely need to know about dogs, baby brothers, soccer, or Florida?"

Throughout this week, continue to add to the writing decisions chart, particularly the "Have Any of Us Tried This?" column (see Figure 3.3).

TITLE AND AUTHOR	WHAT DO WE NOTICE THIS WRITER DOING? (WRITING DECISIONS)	WHY? WHAT EFFECT DOES IT HAVE ON US AS READERS?	NAME IT	HAVE ANY OF US TRIED THIS?
What Does a Garden Need? by Judy Nayer *What Lays Eggs?* by Katherine Gracestone *Who Beats the Heat?* by Pamela Chanko and Daniel Moreton	They give many answers to one question.	It helps us learn how different kinds of things are also sort of the same.	Question–answer– answer–answer	Aidarous did this in his book *Anything That Is Healthy Has Seeds.*
Will We Miss Them? Endangered Species, by Alexandra Wright *What's Under the Log?* by Anne Hunter	They give long answers to their questions.	It tells us all about something, not just a little bit.	Question–a-n-s-w-e-r	Ella did this in *What Is This Animal?*
Baby Animals at Home, by Miriam Frost *What's Inside?* by Colin Walker	They ask different questions and answer each one.	It teaches us about different things that have something in common.	Question–answer– different question– different answer– different question– different answer	Rebecca did this in *What Animals Live Here?*
Where Are the Seeds? by Pauline Cartwright *Seeds, Seeds, Seeds,* by Brian and Jillian Cutting	They ask the same question and give different answers.	It teaches us about different qualities of one thing.	Question–answer– same question– different answer– same question– different answer	Maddie did this in *Holes.*
What's Inside? by Mary Jane Martin *Baby Animals at Home,* by Miriam Frost	They put the answers on the reverse side of the pages containing the questions.	It makes us think a little before we get to see the answer.	Question–think– answer	Daniel did this in *Things That Make You Strong.*

Figure 3.3 *Updated Chart of Nonfiction Question-and-Answer Book Writing Decisions*

Possible Teaching Points

- *Writers of nonfiction choose topics about which they know and care a lot and which make sense to teach others about.* Launch this first nonfiction study of the year by teaching topic choice explicitly. It can be tricky negotiating the fine line between choosing to write about something that is true but not a good topic for nonfiction (e.g., *my mother*) and something that is true and is a good topic *(mothers)*. Rather than try to explain the difference between the personal and the global, encourage children to avoid the personal altogether. In this early lesson, get children thinking about which topics make sense to teach to others: "OK, *my family.* Oh, I know there are a million stories and ideas there, but I don't think it makes sense to teach other people about my family. I can't really see children deciding to read a book that teaches them about *my* mom and *my* dad and *my* sisters and brother. Oh, but look here!

Soccer! Or bike riding! I can really imagine that kids might want to read about either one of those things."

- *Writers think about how they will put their ideas together before they start writing.* Teach children to envision what their books will look and sound like before starting to write them. Show them that if they have a vision of how their books will turn out, they can more easily decide on text structures and formats and find mentor texts.

- *Since this is a book, you might need more pages.* Some children have so many topics they want to write about that they move from one to the next before saying very much. By all means, compliment their enthusiasm and vigor, but help them write as much as they can about a topic before finishing. There is nothing wrong with having a few projects going at a time, but we sell ourselves short when we don't explore topics as fully as possible.

- *Nonfiction writers have to decide which information is most important to teach their readers.* On the other hand, some young writers want to squeeze out every last bit of information before they *allow* themselves to move on to a new topic. Show them how to ask, "Do my readers really need to know that?" If they're writing a book about cheetahs, they don't need to give any information about African snakes. Thinking critically in this way about their own writing helps children make the connection between their ideas and the printed word.

Meeting a Bigger Challenge

This will mean different things for different children. I depend on my conference notes and observations of students' work to tell me how each child can challenge herself or himself appropriately. A challenge for one child might be to spend more time writing about one topic. Another child might take on the challenge of choosing a new topic. In your whole-class minilessons, emphasize the importance of holding oneself to a high standard. In conferences, work with each child to find his or her appropriate level of challenge.

Possible Teaching Points

- *Writers challenge themselves to do the best work they can.* Show children how we sometimes *want* to say, "Well, this will be easy if I do it the way that I already know how. It might not be new or interesting, but it will work out just fine"; however we can learn more if we say instead, "I have a new idea I want to try. It will be hard, and I might not get it right the first time, but it

What is this animal? It is a gazelle.

Figure 3.4 Page of Ella's Book Before Adding Information

Even though gazelles have stripes they are not related to zebras.

Figure 3.5 Ella's Book After Adding Information

will be worth it." Here are some specific ways children might challenge themselves:

- Add more words to each page to elaborate on their topic. (See Ella's writing in Figures 3.4 and 3.5.)
- Add a surprise ending or an ending that changes the pattern. (See Dasha's writing in Figures 3.6 and 3.7.)
- Use a text feature, such as flaps, labels, or captions. (See Rebecca's writing in Figures 3.8 and 3.9.)
- Add an ending that synthesizes the whole book into a sentence or two. (See the last page of Jonathan's seed book in Figure 3.10.)
- Write another kind of nonfiction book. (See the page from Emma's first butterfly book in Figure 3.11.)
- Try a new structure for a familiar topic. (See the page from Emma's second butterfly book in Figure 3.12.)

- ***If writers don't have enough information on their topic, they may need to choose a new topic.*** As you expect children to write more text on each page of

Is there a beach in Florida?

Yes!

Is there an alligator in Florida?

Figure 3.6 End of Dasha's Book Before

Yes!

Is there snow in Florida?

No!

No!

Figure 3.7 Dasha's Book with New Surprise Ending.

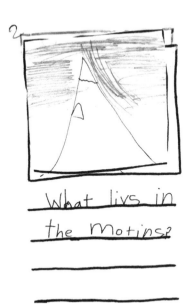

What lives in the mountains?

Figure 3.8 Rebecca's Book with the Flap Down

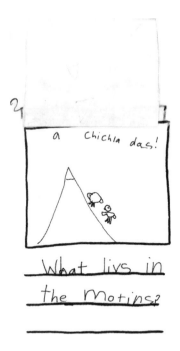

A chinchilla does!

Figure 3.9 Rebecca's Book with the Flap up

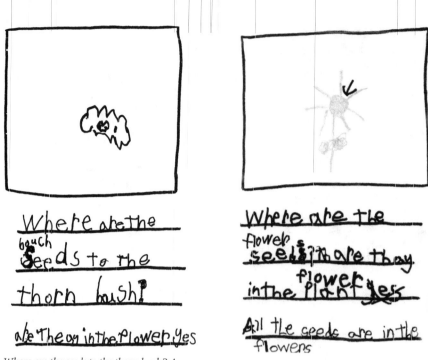

Where are the seeds to the thorn bush? Are they in the flower? Yes.

Where are the flower seeds? Are they in the flower plant? Yes. All the seeds are in the flowers.

Figure 3.10 The Last Pages of Jonathan's Seed Book

their books, you also challenge them to know or find out more about their topics. A child may have written a book about owls that says, "What do owls eat? They eat small animals. When do owls come out? They come out at night." This is perfect if she has been struggling to get words on the paper. But other children can be expected to include much more information about what owls eat and their nocturnal patterns. If a child does not have that information or know where to find it, he may need to switch to a more familiar topic.

- *A writer chooses a structure based on the effect it will have on the reader.* You might encounter children who are having trouble deciding how to organize their questions and answers. This is a perfect opportunity to revisit your writing decisions chart and invite children to think about what effect they want their writing to have on readers. Do they want their readers to have to think before they give an answer? If so, they can make the reader turn the page before seeing the answer. Do they want to give the answer to a question right away? Then they can put it on the same page. Do they want the reader to see something in many ways? Then maybe the whole book can be different

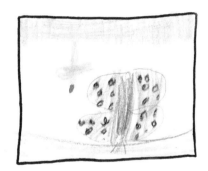

A butterfly redey
to look for
a Place to lay
her eggs

then the
caterpillershatch
they grow
biger bigger.
thenthey climb out of the nest

A butterfly ready to look for a place to lay her eggs . . . then the caterpillars hatch. They grow bigger. Then they climb out of the nest . . .

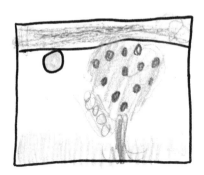

after few days
the caterpilers
go to a tree
to make they
crisalis

they change
inside when
they fly out
they are butterflys

After a few days caterpillars go to a tree to make their chrysalis. They change inside. When they fly out, they are butterflies.

Figure 3.11 Pages from Emma's First Butterfly Book

See that caterpillar? One day it will change into a butterfly. Lets go back to when it was an egg. A butterfly lays her eggs on a leaf. In about two weeks it will hatch into a caterpillar.

FIGURE 3.12 Pages from Emma's Second Butterfly Book

answers to one question. Referring to the chart of writing decisions for ideas of different structures definitely helps build independence by getting children to think deeply about how they are sharing their ideas.

Revising and Editing

In the previous unit of study, you taught children that they could revise by adding more to their ideas. Not everyone will have internalized this strategy. Now you can teach the complementary revision strategy of taking away anything that does not support the idea or the structure of the piece. Possible editing strategies are noticing and correcting backward letters and consulting the word wall in order to spell words correctly.

Possible Teaching Points

- *Nonfiction books usually have titles that tell what the whole book is going to be about.* While children often give their books titles before they make them, a good nonfiction revision strategy is to reevaluate the title they have chosen (or give their book a title if they haven't already). It prompts children to re-read their books and ask themselves what the whole book is about. The ability to sum up a book like this depends on the topic and structure of the book being somewhat consistent.

- *If a word comes up often in your book but is not on the word wall, find the correct spelling somewhere else.* This is particularly helpful in nonfiction. In a minilesson or a conference, demonstrate how you pay attention to particular words that come up often in your work but are not on the word wall. If the book is about candy, the word *candy* is worth looking up so you can spell it correctly every time you write it. Dictionaries can be overwhelming for young writers, so also ask them if they remember seeing the particular word they wish to spell somewhere in the classroom (in a book, for example).

- *Make sure your information is really true.* It's easy to get a little carried away when writing books is so much fun. But a ladybug's spots do not tell how old it is, and the blood inside your body is not blue. This can be tricky. Many times children believe the bizarre "facts" they've written down and therefore don't know what to revise. So instead of asking them to go back to their work and remove information that is not true, I demonstrate how I go back to my own piece of writing and ask myself *Am I sure?* about every page. Whenever I am not sure, I can either remove the information or look it up. (This is not foolproof, by the way. Some of those odd nonfacts will find their way into children's books, but at least you will have taught an important skill.)

Publishing

As you prepare to share your writing, plan a celebration and way of publishing that reflects the big work you have done in this unit. As a community, share your expertise on a variety of topics. You might invite the other first grade classes to your classroom to visit and read your books. To make the visits smoother, group your books on tables, with all topics that are similar or that seem to go together on the same table. The authors can stand nearby to answer any questions readers might have. Celebrating this way is also a great assessment, as the children answer all sorts of questions: "How does the plant start to grow out of the seed?" "How did you decide to make the book have flaps?" "What does that say? I can't read it." Hearing students talk about their work with peers gives you a great window into their thinking.

■ Predictable Problems

When things go wrong, it does not mean we are not doing a good job. We just need to determine the cause of the problem and address it. Some issues that are common in this unit and possible ways to address them follow.

PROBLEM	WHAT IT LOOKS LIKE	POSSIBLE SOLUTION/ CONFERENCE
Children lack confidence or are afraid to take a risk.	• Children write about the same topic that you used in the minilesson. • Children write what seems to be the same book over and over. • Children write only the words they know how to spell.	It is especially important to compliment children who lack confidence. Be on the lookout for things they do well, because they will know if your compliment is authentic. Remind them of some of the things they know and care an awful lot about. They might not realize how much they know!
Children choose uninteresting or inappropriate topics.	• Children write a page or two but cannot think of more to write on the topic. • Children write information in their books that is not true.	Reteach the minilesson about choosing topics.
Children don't yet have a strong grasp of the question-and-answer structure.	• The pages in a book do not follow a consistent pattern. • The information in a book is not parallel from page to page.	First, be patient. Then, ask children how the pages go together. They might point out something you did not see. If they do have trouble saying how the pages go together, you can ask them how they would like to make the pages match better. Then, help them follow through.
Children are not meeting new challenges.	• Folders contain lots of writing, but all of it seems to be exactly the same. • Children are becoming bored. • You are becoming bored.	Have lots of published books on hand that can provide a vision for how the children's books can look. Create some books in shared or interactive writing that break away from a too-predictable structure.
Your teaching is not reaching all learners.	• More advanced students do not appear to be working at their full potential. • Students who struggle with the work seem unengaged.	Make sure you have mentor texts appropriate to the range of ability levels in your class. Try conferring with struggling children a few extra times; they may need more individualized teaching until they have a better idea of what they can expect from themselves.

Assessment

The students' published work is just one window into what they have learned. You also need to review your goals for the unit and consider how your students are meeting those goals. The rubric in Figure 3.13 will help you plan whole-group, small-group, and individual instruction in upcoming units of study (learning from a mentor author, genres, or revision, for example).

As you pull together children's published pieces, look especially at how they work with structure. Although structure is necessary in everything they write, you may not be focusing on it so intently during the next several months. Keep track of who will need extra, individualized help during the remaining units of study.

	1 RARELY	2 SOMETIMES	3 MOST OF THE TIME	4 MORE THAN I EXPECT
WRITING QUALITY				
Child writes with an authoritative or knowledgeable voice; his/her word choice and sentence structure reflect knowledge of the topic.	❏	❏	❏	❏
Child makes conscious decisions about text structure.	❏	❏	❏	❏
Child uses a text structure and topic consistently through a whole piece of writing.	❏	❏	❏	❏
Child is able to name the topic of her/his books, giving each a title or cover blurb that describes the content of the whole book in a few words.	❏	❏	❏	❏
Child is able to tell how an individual page connects to the topic of the whole book.	❏	❏	❏	❏
WRITING HABITS				
Child chooses topics that he/she knows and cares a great deal about and that make sense as nonfiction topics.	❏	❏	❏	❏
Child reads and rereads everything she/he writes.	❏	❏	❏	❏
Child revises her/his work, with support and encouragement.	❏	❏	❏	❏
WRITING CONVENTIONS				
Child puts spaces between his/her words (may still use dashes for this).	❏	❏	❏	❏
Child forms letters correctly and in the proper case.	❏	❏	❏	❏
Child spells correctly any words that are on the word wall.	❏	❏	❏	❏
COMMUNITY				
Child is aware of which topics many of his/her peers have chosen.	❏	❏	❏	❏
Child is able to make some smart decisions about which peers to ask for help with different writing issues.	❏	❏	❏	❏
Child shares books and observations about books with classmates.	❏	❏	❏	❏
Child asks questions about and compliments classmates' work.	❏	❏	❏	❏

Figure 3.13 *Pattern Book Assessment Rubric*

4 | Personal Narrative

A
s you approach the end of the school year, your students' writing should look and sound different—longer, clearer, easier to read—because they have been learning so much about structuring and planning texts, using amazing and specific language, finding their voices, and living in a community of writers. This unit harnesses all of these skills as you teach children to write clear and well-structured stories about meaningful experiences in their lives.

A narrative recounts events, tells a story. The forms of narrative are varied and complex, and your students will be ready to write in any and all of them in the future if you set them up with some basic principles now. For the purposes of this unit, I am using a simple and straightforward definition of *narrative:* a single important event told chronologically as a sequence of moments. In other words, the personal narratives in this unit will be stories, not just verbal snapshots.

While most people agree that stories have certain ingredients, there are many opinions about what these are. Here's my list:

- *Plot:* The things that happen in the story, in order. Plot often involves a problem and its resolution, causing some kind of change in a character or characters.

- *Characters:* The people or animals in the story.

- *Setting:* Where and when the story takes place.

Children will be able to use these elements more easily in writing if they learn about them first in reading. Before starting to write personal narratives with your students, you need to spend some time reading stories aloud, discussing the elements found in a story, and teaching the children how these elements work together to make a story. Choose stories that are good models for the kinds of writing you hope your children will do.

■ Overview

This unit is about four weeks long. Throughout, you will continue to read the mentor books you've chosen, shifting your focus from reading as readers to reading as writers. You'll look at how authors structure their stories and how they use language (words, sentences, punctuation, etc.). It is vital to teach children to *tell* their stories well before teaching them to *write* them well. I always begin this unit with oral storytelling, which allows children to revise their work instantly, trying out several possible structures or ways of using detail. (If they had to write each attempt, it would take days to do the work you can accomplish in just one oral session.) At the end of this first week, children publish a wordless book, which they share by telling the story orally as they turn its pages. If you feel uncomfortable with wordless books, have children write a brief synopsis of each part of the story on the appropriate page. This will help them remember key events or details in their stories but does not replace the oral retelling, which ideally will be richer, more complex, and more detailed than what they have written.

Again, there is so much you *could* teach the students in this unit, but you must be disciplined so that you don't overwhelm them. Examine your goals for the year and choose the few things that will help them the most. You want children to be able to write several pages about single significant events. Specifically, you'll teach them ways to use words thoughtfully, play with how time passes, use dialogue, and consider their audience. You'll also refer to the previous work on structuring texts, helping children plan their stories before they start to write them so that each story will wind a beautiful path from beginning to end. Planning a story in its entirety before starting to write it is much harder than planning a list. Bringing your students closer to doing this independently requires many small steps, first orally, then with pictures, and finally with words.

■ Goals

As you approach the end of the year, your unit goals will more closely resemble your goals for the year. Keep the finish line in clear view as you plan and teach. However, since you are concentrating on narrative structures, many of your particular goals will have to do with the specific qualities of this type of writing.

Writing Quality

Children will:

- Write clear, engaging narratives.

- Write stories about single significant events.

- Use a variety of kinds of sentences.

- Think about which words to use to say exactly what they mean to say.

- Show, not tell, characters' feelings.

- Use some of the techniques for developing a story in writing: adding dialogue, adding thoughts or feelings, adding sensory information, and so on.

Writing Habits

Children will:

- Tell stories that have significance and are engaging.

- Plan stories orally before starting to write them.

- Reread their stories often, thinking about how best to tell them.

- Try writing techniques they have encountered in books.

Writing Conventions

Children will:

- Learn to use quotation marks properly.

- Correctly spell more frequently used words.

Community

Children will:

- Be aware of which stories many of their peers have chosen to tell or write.

- With a partner, tell and respond to stories orally before writing them.

- Be able to make some informed decisions about which peers to ask for help with what.

- Suggest possible passages from books for classmates to use as mentor texts.

■ Getting Ready to Teach

In the months since the nonfiction question-and-answer unit, you will have moved on from text structure as an explicit focus and worked on other qualities of good writing, such as building good habits, studying an author or a genre, using language in specific and honest ways, and using writing conventions properly. As you approach the end of the school year, it makes sense to take a closer look at your overall goals. You need to consider your recent work as it relates to your goals for the end of the year, planning lessons and choosing materials that will help you meet those goals.

Considering the Students

The most important influence on planning this unit is the students themselves. Look carefully at everything they have written so far, including poetry and nonfiction. Poems, in particular, are often short, and you may need to help children rebuild the stamina needed to work on a single piece of writing over time. If this is the first narrative writing your students have done in a while, warm children up to what a story is before launching headlong into the genre. Spend time getting them used to it again. Tell and read aloud a lot of stories at the beginning of the unit.

Gathering Books

Gather the books for this study weeks ahead of time so that you will be very familiar with them and can discuss them in depth. A class library has hundreds of stories in it, and it can be hard to choose five or six as mentor texts. I narrow down my choices using the following criteria:

1. I have to love each book I choose. The children aren't going to care deeply about the books if I don't. When I love the books I read to my students, I model how writers learn from the books in their own libraries.

2. I have to be able to name several things the book will help me teach about writing good narratives. I must have a vision for how this book can fuel my lessons and conferences.

3. The stories must be ones I can imagine my students writing about their own lives. I stay away from fantasies and quests, instead picking stories that more closely resemble my students' lives. I choose stories in which the characters have to deal with problems a six-year-old might have experienced, like sibling rivalry, getting into trouble, or being scared to go to school on the first day.

Once I have identified several things I can teach in each of the books I have chosen, I find the specific passages and name the specific strategies or techniques they exemplify. This means reading with sticky notes at hand, jotting down the strategy or quality of writing and the page number and placing the note inside the back cover of the book. (A list of books with possible teaching ideas is included in Appendix A.)

Making Paper

In the first days of the unit, children tell and retell oral stories from their lives using three fingers to delineate the individual moments. I give them paper that has three boxes (one for each finger) with a few lines beneath each box (see Appendix B). When they choose one story to publish as a wordless book, they cut the sections apart and staple them together inside a construction paper cover.

As they get stronger at telling stories with more information and better-developed plots, I teach them how to stretch their stories across five fingers. I demonstrate telling the middle part of my story in greater detail while keeping the beginning and end essentially the same. They then use two sheets of the three-box paper to hold their stories, and the extra box becomes a title page or is just left blank. (The blank boxes are saved in the writing center and used when someone wants to add pages to a book.)

Later in the unit, as children tell their stories orally as a way to plan how their writing will go, they can use the same three-box paper to hold their plans for their written stories.

When they are ready to write their stories based on the plans they have made, I provide two kinds of full-sheet writing paper. Both have room for a picture and words, but one is oriented vertically, the other horizontally, so children can choose how they want the final product to look.

▣ Teaching

Like each earlier unit, this one begins with reading like writers. Children listen to and read stories, paying special attention to decisions writers make and the effects those decisions have on readers. The section on telling and planning stories may be new to your writing workshop. In it, you show children how to tell their stories well. You'll teach a couple of storytelling strategies, coaching the children to revise often until their stories are full and rich yet focused. You'll continue to teach strategies for elaborating on, or stretching, their stories as they write and revise. Before publishing, the children will reflect on their new knowledge of story structure so that you can better meet their needs in the next unit. A table depicting the unit at a glance is shown in Figure 4.1.

Reading Like Writers

By now children are used to beginning a new study in writing workshop by looking at the work of people who have gone before. You have spent a few weeks reading great stories and have chosen a few favorites that will become your mentor texts. Your students know these stories well and are now ready to turn them inside out and look at how they are made. You will continue this

TIME (A GENERAL GUIDELINE)	SECTION OF STUDY	WHAT NEEDS TO BE DONE IN THIS SECTION? CHILDREN WILL:
Ongoing	Reading Like Writers	• Discuss how some of their favorite stories are written and structured. • Categorize the topics these stories address. • Look specifically at leads and categorize them.
4–5 days	Telling and Planning Stories	• Choose an important story to tell. • Practice telling the story as a sequence of events with a central plot line. • Revise how they tell the story by telling different parts with varying amounts of detail. • Give feedback to storytellers and accept feedback from listeners (mostly classmates) about how to make the story more engaging. • Publish a wordless book accompanied by an oral telling of the story.
7–8 days	Developing Our Stories in Writing	• Make plans for a few stories, using sketches and oral storytelling. • Use their plans to help write the stories. • Try some craft elements that they have noticed in published books. • Add to the personal narrative writing decisions chart, noticing which students in the class have tried different techniques.
5–6 days	Revising and Editing	• Choose a story to publish. • Revise the story using the revision strategies checklist, including one new item: stretching important parts of the story. • Add a new strategy to the editing checklist: circling words that don't look right and trying alternative spellings.
2 days	Publication, Reflection, and Assessment	• Complete a self-assessment questionnaire. • Celebrate!

Figure 4.1 *Personal Narrative at a Glance*

BOOK	WHAT KIND OF STORY IS THIS?	WHAT DO WE NOTICE THIS WRITER DOING?	WHY? WHAT EFFECT DOES IT HAVE ON US AS READERS?	NAME IT	HAVE ANY OF US TRIED THIS?
The Hating Book, by Charlotte Zolotow	The character has to grow up or change a little.	She starts with a strong feeling.	It puts us right in the middle of the story.	Starting with a bang	
Owl Babies, by Martin Waddell	You think something really bad is going to happen, but it all turns out OK.	Some words are in all capital letters.	Those words seem more important. We read them with stronger voices.	Strong words	
Shortcut, by Donald Crews	You think something really bad is going to happen, but it all turns out OK.	He makes some words bigger than others. He tells the scary part through what the characters say to one another.	We read bigger words louder. It makes us feel like we are really there.	Loud words Dialogue	
The Kissing Hand, by Audrey Penn	The first time or last time something happened.	She tells some parts with a lot more detail than other parts.	It makes these parts stand out. It gives us a picture in our minds of what is happening. These parts feel slow.	Slowing the story down	

Figure 4.2 *Personal Narrative Writing Decisions*

process throughout the unit, adding to the writing decisions chart (see Figure 4.2) as you go. (The chart now includes a specific column in which to record what kind of story it is.) I always point out that many of the best stories involve some kind of trouble. The characters grapple with their problems and often change somehow as a result.

Telling and Planning Stories

In this section, you'll teach children about oral storytelling through whole-group guided practice. You'll still demonstrate and give examples of the concepts you are teaching, but you'll spend a lot more time working with the class as a group, perhaps asking students to turn and talk with a partner while you listen in or asking specific children to try telling their story to the whole group while you coach them. You'll show them how to be the storyteller, the listener, and the coach, so that they will be able to support one another when they are working independently. Listen in on the following vignette:

STEPHANIE: Everybody, come on over here. Let's sit in a circle instead of a clump today for writing workshop. Today is a special day. We are starting a new unit! For the next few weeks, we're going to be telling and writing the stories of our lives that matter to us the most. We're going to share with the world the stories that have made us who we are today. Think about that for a minute. Think about all the things that have happened to you in your life that have really made a difference.

HENRY: You mean, like when I got my scar?

STEPHANIE: Exactly. You'll never forget that, will you?

HANA: [*laughing*] I'll never forget the time me and my mom and my brother and Neil went on a bike ride and got caught in the rain!

STEPHANIE: Ooh, I can't wait to hear that one!

And so begins the journey toward telling these stories *well.*

Storytelling is vital to the writing lives of children and an important part of this unit. You may be tempted to skip it, but it pays not to. Many teachers (and principals) are uncomfortable with the idea that children are "just talking" for a week of writing workshop. They are doing so much more than just talking, though! Through oral storytelling, they are learning which stories are worth telling, how to tell a story in a way that engages the audience, how to sequence the events and describe the details of the story for maximum effect, which events and details to leave out altogether, and how to speed up or slow down time to keep an audience interested. Students can tell a story one way, listen to feedback, and try telling it differently in the space of about ten minutes. In a single workshop period (about forty minutes), a child might revise an oral retelling of a story four or five times. Children probably could learn all of this through writing and revising their stories, but it would take longer and they would experience a lot more frustration.

I teach children to tell their stories across three (and later, five) fingers, a strategy I learned from my colleagues at the Teachers College Reading and Writing Project. This helps children visualize how the story is moving through time as they tell it. To demonstrate, I tell a story, touching successive fingers (starting with the thumb) at each turning point in the story. Just what constitutes a turning point can be difficult for young storytellers to grasp. Many children think everything is a turning point and go through all five fingers before anything has happened. Others lump separate moments together or include so few that they reach the end on just two fingers.

At the conclusion of this section, each child makes a wordless book—or one with just a few words on a page—to accompany his or her retelling of the story.

At first, these wordless books will have three, four, or five pages—one for each finger of the story. Later, as they get stronger at telling stories well, children can break away from this convention. The wordless book helps the writer remember the structure of the story, so that he can tell it pretty much the same way every time he shares the story. (In the next section of the study, you'll use similar wordless books as plans, or foundations, for the stories that your students will soon be writing.)

Possible Teaching Points

- *The writers we love tell stories that matter. We can study these to learn how we can tell stories that matter.* It can be hard for children to figure out which of the many experiences they've had in their lives will make great stories. One way is to learn from the books in the classroom library, studying the kinds of stories *their* authors tell. Help children discover that all of the great books you will be working with this month tell a story of how the writer or main character has changed in some way. Maybe he or she learned lessons, faced adversity, or just had to grow up a little. The writing decisions chart of the kinds of stories your class is reading is a good reference for helping children think of great stories from their own lives.

- *When we tell a story across three fingers, we can start by saying where we were and who was with us. I'm going to call that* **setting the scene.** *Then we can tell about the problem or the thing that made us have to change. Finally, we can tell how it all worked out.* These are a lot of steps, so children are going to need a clear demonstration and lots of coaching. I make sure I have a couple of stories from my own life ready to use as examples throughout the unit. I come back to these stories again and again as I teach children new skills for developing their own stories. I might say, "So as I hold up my first finger, I say where I was and who I was with and maybe even what we were doing. Listen. 'I went to the grocery store with my mother. We were in the cereal aisle. I was looking at all the sugary cereals.' OK, now I'm ready for the next finger. Here is where I tell what the problem was or what made me have to change. 'I looked to the side. My mother was gone! I was alone!' Now I am ready for my last finger. This is where we find out how it all ends up. 'After a while I heard her voice calling my name. I was found!' Now let's try that with one of your stories." It's important that children try telling their stories while the other children listen so that everyone benefits from your coaching and support. The vignette in Figure 4.3 is an example of how this might go. Though these stories may seem short or stark, if the children have

Figure 4.3 *Three-Fingers Vignette*

the three fingers of their stories in place and focused, they have the raw material to develop some great stories.

- *We can make our stories more interesting and clear by saying more about the problem or the thing that made us have to change. We may need to use all five fingers!* Here you want to focus on the interior sections of students' stories. First demonstrate and then coach children as they lengthen their stories from within by making the middle part last longer. I use the same story or couple of stories to demonstrate all these strategies so the children can see how each strategy changes the story. "Today I am going to show you how I can say more about the problem of my story. Remember yesterday on my second finger I said, 'I looked to the side. My mother was gone! I was alone!' Now listen to how I can tell you so much more about that moment. 'I turned to the side to ask my mom if we could get some Count Chocula. But she wasn't there! The aisle was empty.' I need another finger for this. 'I looked up the other way and she wasn't there either. I looked back again.' Oh, goodness, I need one more finger. 'I called out to her, but there was no answer. I was alone.' I have only one finger left, so now it's time for the end of my story." The vignette in Figure 4.4 is an example of public coaching to help a student stretch her story.

- *We need to think about where our stories begin and end.* I am often guilty of starting my narratives a long way before the story's point. For some reason, I'm afraid my readers won't get it unless I tell them about the whole week leading up to the main events. Many students have this habit too, as well as the companion habit of needing to end their stories with "And then I went to bed and slept and then I woke up the next day and ate breakfast." When my friend Semi Chellas, writer and producer of the award-winning Canadian newsroom drama *The Eleventh Hour,* was a little girl, her mother taught her

Stephanie:	Jackie, let's look at the second finger of your story.
Jackie:	Oh, I get it. I was driving in the car with my mom, and I was sitting in my old car seat. OK, here's the second finger. It was small and I felt babyish. When we got home, my mom ordered a new one from the computer. I waited for it. Then—
Stephanie:	How did you behave while you waited for it?
Jackie:	Every day after school I asked my mom if it was there yet.
Stephanie:	Nice! You really told us more about the second finger. Keep going.
Jackie:	Then finally one day it came. My mom buckled me in and I felt more grown up.
Stephanie:	Did you guys all hear the difference between Jackie's two stories? One was sort of ho-hum and the other was getting pretty juicy. The more information she included, the more we enjoyed her story.

Jackie's oral story before:

I was driving in the car with my mom, and I was sitting in my old car seat. It was small. I felt kind of babyish. Then we got a new one. It came in the mail.

Jackie's oral story after:

I was driving in the car with my mom, and I was sitting in my old car seat. It was small and I felt babyish. When we got home, my mom ordered a new from the computer. I waited for it. Every day after school I asked my mom if it was there yet. Then finally one day it came. My mom buckled me in and I felt more grown up.

Figure 4.4 *Public Coaching Vignette*

about story through the metaphor of a string: "Think of your life as a string. As a writer, you hold the scissors! You can cut the exact segment of string that you want your readers to experience." This metaphor creates a very clear image of the stories we *tell* as being a small portion of the stories we *live*. I use it to show children how to make conscious choices about where in time to begin and end their stories: "My grocery store story used to go like this. 'One day I was playing outside. My mom told me to get in the car. We went to the grocery store. We were in the cereal aisle.' And then you know the rest. The part about playing doesn't go with the part about getting lost. It just doesn't fit. So I can take my scissors and snip it off! Even though it really happened that day, I don't have to have it in my story!"

- *We need to plan how our story will go on paper before we can write it.* Children often tell fantastic stories on their fingers but then write something totally different on their paper. It's hard for them to keep a story intact in their minds while they are concentrating on drawing and writing. Touching each box on the paper as they tell each finger of the story helps them make the transition from oral to written story. Demonstrate by telling the first finger of your story as you physically touch the first box on the paper. Then move your next finger to the next box as you tell the next part of the story.

Developing Our Stories in Writing

In this section, students continue to practice telling stories across their fingers and making wordless books, but these books now become plans for the stories they will write. You'll teach them how to use each page of the wordless book as a foundation for a page in a full-size (8½-by-11-inch) book. The simplest way is to cut apart the plan and tape each piece to a separate piece of writing paper. (Figure 4.5 contains my original three-part plan for the grocery store story as well as my fleshed-out middle section; Figure 4.6 is that plan transferred to a booklet.)

Most of your teaching, though, will now be about qualities of good writing. Students will need to add a lot of elaboration to their plans in order to make them into rich stories. A long time ago—before I began to demonstrate or give examples in every minilesson and conference—I used to tell my students to add details to their writing. I now understand how vague this advice was, that I needed to be specific about the *kinds* of details that might help the writing. In particular, this is a good time to teach children about revealing how a character might be feeling and about using dialogue to help tell the story. Also, show them how to look at the qualities of the writing in the mentor texts and how to try those in their own writing. Teach students who seem ready how to stretch one important part of their story, or one page, across two or three pages—how to slow down time so that the reader can spend more time reading about the important parts.

Possible ways to develop, or stretch, stories include the following:

- Add characters' thoughts or feelings.

- Include what characters see, hear, smell, taste, and feel.

- Let the reader hear characters talking (dialogue).

- Give a blow-by-blow account (tell everything that happened in a part of the story).

- Find the most important part, or heart, of the story and say more about it.

- Make sure details that are in the pictures are also in the words (for example, if characters are smiling in the picture, write that in the words, too).

- Add a new beginning or ending.

- Tell about the setting.

Figure 4.5 *My Original Three-Part Story Plan and My Stretched-Out Problem*

Figure 4.6 *My Model Plan Transferred to a Booklet*

Possible Teaching Points

● ***When we use our plan to help us write, we can write the words that go with the picture on each page.*** Later in their writing lives, children will learn about things like *rising action* and *denouement,* but for now the three- or five-finger approach will achieve the goal of a structure that engages the listener and reader. Make sure the words they write for each section of the story matches the plan they have made. If a writer tells all there is to tell about a section of his story but there are still lines on that page, he need not keep writing to fill the page. Instead, he can turn to a new page and write *that* section of the story.

● ***Sometimes writers let their readers know what they are thinking or feeling in their stories.*** Using carets or sticky notes, demonstrate adding what is going on inside you as the events of your story are unfolding: "In this part of the story I was thinking that I really wanted some Count Chocula. I'm going to add the words *I really wanted some* to this page. Now, I'll keep reading. Oh, I remember here I was feeling scared. I'm going to add the words *I was scared.*" Teaching children to include internal as well as external information about the characters in their stories helps them make deeper connections with their readers.

● ***Sometimes writers let their readers hear the characters talking in their stories.*** If a story involves a number of people, chances are good that they spoke to one another. Show children how you write dialogue: "Let me think back to that day when I got lost. I remember calling for my mom, so I can put in the words *'Mom,' I called.* And of course I have to remember to put quotation marks around the exact thing I said, so I'll put them before and after *Mom.*" Again, show them how to use symbols like carets or stars so that their additions don't get too confusing.

● ***Writers can make their readers feel as if they are in the story by showing them what the characters see.*** One strategy for adding sensory information to a story is to show the reader what the character sees. When you demonstrate this, let the children see that you're adding things that enrich the story, not just random information: "Now I'm going to let my readers see what I saw in the grocery store that day. I could add all the boxes of cereal and the price tags, but that doesn't really help my story. It does help my story if I tell you that I looked both ways, up and down, and just saw the empty aisle with no Mom standing there. That information is important to my story."

- *Writers revise all the time, not just when someone tells them to. They think about all the revision strategies they know and try the ones they think might help.* Demonstrate that one thing to do when they feel stuck is to look at the revision checklist and try strategies that might help them tell their stories better. Don't emphasize any particular strategy, just how important it is to use the chart as a resource.

Revising and Editing

Although some children are no doubt already revising and editing their writing, this is the point at which you'll teach a new strategy to add to each checklist. Particularly helpful for narrative writing is having a strong beginning and a satisfying ending. Invite the children to join you in investigating the different sorts of endings in the mentor stories and charting your findings (see Figure 4.7). (You'll deal with beginnings in the next unit, on fiction.) A new editing strategy is to circle words that do not look right and try a couple of alternate spellings.

Possible Teaching Points

- *We can try to end our stories like our favorite authors do.* Charting the kinds of beginnings and endings authors use in their stories reveals that endings tend to be some kind of wrap-up—looking ahead, looking back, or commenting on the experience. These terms are pretty fancy for first graders; you'll need to demonstrate all three kinds of endings so that the children can

TITLE	HOW DOES THIS BOOK END?	HAVE ANY OF US TRIED THIS?
The Hating Book by Charlotte Zolotow	Looking forward: "I wish it were tomorrow."	
Big Sister and Little Sister by Charlotte Zolotow	Looking forward: "And from that day on . . ."	
Owl Babies by Martin Waddell	Commenting on the experience: "'I knew it,' said Sarah. 'And I knew it!' said Percy. 'I love my mommy!' said Bill."	
Shortcut by Donald Crews	Looking back on the experience: "We didn't talk about what happened for a very long time. And we didn't take the shortcut again."	

Figure 4.7 *Personal Narrative Endings*

see how they work and choose for themselves how best to end their stories. Looking ahead: "From now on I will always make sure to stay right next to my mom." Looking back: "I never got lost in the grocery store again." Commenting on the experience: "Even though I was scared, I knew my mom would come find me."

- *It can be powerful to show, rather than tell, how a character is feeling.* You've already encouraged children to let their readers know how their characters are feeling at different points in their stories. Take that idea one step further and teach them to create an image of what that feeling might look like. Show children a piece of your own writing in which you've told how you felt: "I was sad." Then close your eyes and imagine the physical experience of that emotion: "So, when I felt sad, I remember that I didn't want to cry, but I could feel a lump in my throat and my eyes were burning. So I will cross out 'I felt sad' and write, 'I felt a lump in my throat and my eyes started to burn' in its place."

- *All the words we have learned should be spelled correctly, and so should the blends and spelling patterns we know.* Children already know that any words they learn in spelling or word study should always be spelled correctly in their published work. Now teach them that if they know a lot of words, they also know a lot of *parts* of words. If, for instance, they know how to spell *from* and *name,* they also know how to spell *frame.* Have the children look through their writing for parts of words they have learned, fixing spelling where necessary.

- *When we write dialogue, we must use quotation marks correctly.* It's easier to teach this lesson if you liken quotation marks to speech bubbles. I tell children, "When you use speech bubbles, you draw a circle just around the words people are saying. You wouldn't write *he said* in the speech bubble because the character is not saying *he said.* Quotation marks, or talking marks, work the same way. They hold only the words people are saying in your story. If you want to write *he said,* you can put that *outside* the quotation marks." As with any other new things they are learning, children will approximate this before they master it.

It can be hard to imagine how these teaching points translate into children's writing. Aidan's story (Figure 4.8) will help you envision what you may expect from your own class. Figure 4.9 details how Aidan uses the strategies he has learned.

Me and dad
went to the
bech ner the curent.
I thot if I fel in I
wad shoerly drown. I
woct a way.

Later my frands
went ner the curent
I desiydid to go
with them. My
brather came with me.
I shud
have stdyd away from
the curent.

Me and Dad went to the beach near the current. I thought if I fell in I would surely drown. I walked away.

Later my friends went near the current. I decided to go with them. My brother came with me. I should have stayed away from the current.

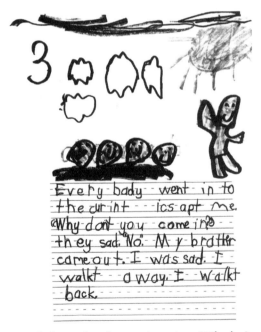

Every bady went in to
the curint ics apt me.
Why don't you come in?
they sad. No. My brather
came out. I was sad. I
walkt away. I walkt
back.

Boom! I fell in! My
brather pasht me in.
I was v are hot.

Everybody went into the current except me. "Why don't you come in?" they said. "No." My brother came out. I was sad. I walked away. I walked back.

Boom! I fell in! My brother pushed me in. I was very hot.

Figure 4.8 *Aidan's Story,* The Current

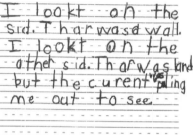

I looked on the side. There was a wall. I looked on the other side. There was land but the current was pulling me out to sea.

I did not know what to do. I was getting farther and farther away. I tried to swim to shore but the current was too strong.

My friends did not know what to do. My throat was dry. I was breathing hard. "We will ask your dad to help you," said my friends.

I felt scared. Suddenly I felt something holding on to me. I looked up. I am saved, but who is this? Dad! Ha I am saved!

Figure 4.8 *Aidan's Story,* The Current *(continued)*

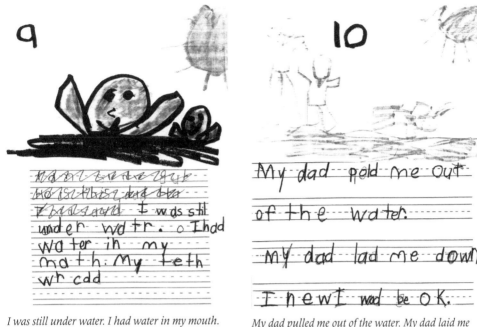

I was still under water. I had water in my mouth.
My teeth were cold.

My dad pulled me out of the water. My dad laid me
down. I knew I would be OK.

Figure 4.8 *(continued)*

Publication, Reflection, and Assessment

As children finish their stories, they can add covers, cover blurbs, or about-the-author pieces and color their illustrations. (Children who finish just in the nick of time may have only enough time to add a cover.) One or two times in a year, it's a nice touch to laminate the pages of children's books and bind the pages together (if your school has a spiral binder). This takes some additional time, but it makes this publication stand out as something special. I am usually so impressed with the writing children produce in this unit (after nearly a year of instruction) that I go to great lengths to make their books, and our celebration, something that they and their families will remember for a long time.

It's also nice to give children a chance to read their stories aloud, since they have been working on fluency and phrasing in reading workshop. They can read their own work with so much more attention to sound and meaning than they could in the beginning of the year. It takes too long to have everyone read the same day, but they could read to the other children at their table (with all the tables reading simultaneously), or four or five children can read their stories each day during publication week.

WRITING STRATEGY	HOW IT APPEARS IN AIDAN'S STORY
Include what characters see, hear, smell, taste, and feel.	I looked on the side. There was a wall. I looked on the other side. There was land but the current was pulling me out to sea. I tried to swim to shore but the current was too strong. Suddenly I felt something holding on to me. My teeth were cold.
Add what the character thinks or wonders.	I thought if I fell in I would surely drown. I should have stayed away from the current. I am saved, but who is this? I knew I would be OK.
Add characters' feelings.	I was sad. I was very hot.
Let the reader hear characters talking (dialogue).	"Why don't you come in?" "We will ask your dad to help you."
Show, not tell, feelings.	I walked away. I walked back. My throat was dry. I was breathing hard.
Give a blow-by-blow account (tell everything that happened in a part of the story).	I looked on the side. There was a wall. I looked on the other side. There was land but the current was pulling me out to sea. I did not know what to do. I was getting farther and farther away. I tried to swim to shore but the current was too strong. I was still under water. I had water in my mouth. My teeth were cold. My dad pulled me out of the water. My dad laid me down.

Figure 4.9 How Aidan Uses the Strategies He Has Learned

◼ Predictable Problems

When things go wrong, it does not mean we are not doing a good job. We just need to determine the cause of the problem and address it. Some issues that are common in this unit and possible ways to address them follow.

PROBLEM	WHAT IT LOOKS LIKE	POSSIBLE SOLUTION/ CONFERENCE
Children lack confidence or are afraid to take a risk.	• Children write the same story you modeled in the lesson. • Children cannot think of anything to write. • Children say that they have no stories to tell. • Children write stories about movies they have seen or video games they enjoy.	It is especially important to compliment children who lack confidence. Be on the lookout for things they do well because they will know if your compliment is authentic. Remind them of some of the stories they have told you about their families or their weekends or their interests outside of school.

Children's stories are boring.	• Children write stories about movies they have seen or video games they enjoy. • Children tell stories in which nothing really happens.	Try not to let your frustration show. Children sometimes believe these are the only things worth telling stories about. Speak to them as if their lives really matters in this classroom. Sometimes letting a child write one of these stories gets it out of his system and he can move on to more fertile ground. Also, choose stories to read aloud that validate the importance of things that happen in their lives.
Children are unsure of how to communicate the significance of their stories in their lives.	• Children tell stories that do not seem to have significance. • Children spend more time on the minor details and only briefly touch on the heart of their stories.	Sometimes children tell a story that matters deeply to them, but they leave out the part that matters most. Your first instinct might be to ask for tons of specific details or to persuade the child to find a new topic. If you give yourself the chance, though, you can mine the diamond inside the rough story. Respond to the child as if you know she has an important reason for telling this story above all others, and show her how to tell a story so that the important parts show rather than remain hidden.
Stories are not told as sequences of events or don't use story language.	• The story is like one long sentence with a lot of "and then . . . and then . . ." language. • The story seems to be more like a day-in-the-life piece than a story about one thing.	Address this in your oral storytelling work. Model telling your own stories sequentially and with significant information included. Point out how you do not tell your story as one long sentence with "and then" between every part. Instead, you speak in sentences. When you allow children to hear the difference between these two ways of telling a story, it will be easier for them to tell their own stories better. This will in turn improve their written stories.

■ Assessment

When you look at your students' writing at the end of this unit, focus specifically on things that pertain to their understanding of narrative and their grasp of qualities of good writing. For example, pay attention to how well students are able to focus and sequence a story. As you review unit goals, look at how children are reaching or approaching your expectations. As always, look for individual needs as well as patterns to help you plan for lessons, conferences, or small-group work in the next unit. A suggested assessment rubric is shown in Figure 4.10.

I am very interested in children's perceptions of this unit. A self-assessment sheet (Figure 4.11) lets me know what they have learned, what they understand about narrative, and what parts of the process they have internalized.

WRITING QUALITY	1 RARELY	2 SOMETIMES	3 MOST OF THE TIME	4 MORE THAN I EXPECT
Child writes engaging stories about single significant events.	❏	❏	❏	❏
Child tries to show characters' feelings with dialogue or action, instead of just telling what the feelings are.	❏	❏	❏	❏
Child uses a variety of kinds of sentences.	❏	❏	❏	❏
Child thinks about which words to use to say exactly what he/she means to say.	❏	❏	❏	❏
Child uses a few techniques for developing a story in writing: adding dialogue, adding thoughts or feelings, adding sensory information, and so on.	❏	❏	❏	❏
WRITING HABITS				
Child tells stories that have significance and are engaging.	❏	❏	❏	❏
Child plans stories before starting to write.	❏	❏	❏	❏
Child reads and rereads her/his stories, thinking about how best to tell them.	❏	❏	❏	❏
Child tries writing techniques he/she has seen in books.	❏	❏	❏	❏
Child has a vision for how she/he wants her/his story to go and revises often to achieve this.	❏	❏	❏	❏
WRITING CONVENTIONS				
Child uses quotation marks correctly.	❏	❏	❏	❏
Child forms letters correctly and in the proper case.	❏	❏	❏	❏
Child spells between seventy and ninety frequently used words correctly.	❏	❏	❏	❏
COMMUNITY				
Child is aware of which topics many of his/her peers have chosen.	❏	❏	❏	❏
Child is able to make some smart decisions about which peers to ask for help with different writing issues.	❏	❏	❏	❏
Child shares books and observations about books with classmates.	❏	❏	❏	❏
Child asks questions about and compliments classmates' work.	❏	❏	❏	❏

Figure 4.10 *Personal Narrative Assessment Rubric*

Name _____ Date _____

Congratulations! You have worked hard on your stories and now they are finished.

What new thing did you learn about how stories go?

_____

_____

_____

_____

Which strategies did you use to stretch your story?

_____

_____

_____

If you wanted to write a story right now, how would you start?

_____

_____

_____

_____

Figure 4.11 *Personal Narrative Self-Assessment Sheet*

5 | Fiction

This unit can be very rewarding, but get ready to do some work! It takes a strong will to dissuade children from writing about alien attacks or child secret agents. Not that I have anything against fantasy, but it is more difficult to do well than realistic fiction. Of course, any kind of fiction is easy to write badly, but that's something you can use to your advantage. Why is it easy for children to write fiction badly? Because they want to write it and approach it with a lot of enthusiasm and drama (the *easy* part) but have just a budding knowledge of how to structure a story well (the *badly* part). So all you have to do is channel all that enthusiasm and drama into learning about structure, and voila! Great stories! Well, maybe it won't be *that* simple, but it's springtime, so make sure to have a good time.

In this unit you'll add some strategies for plot development to the students' repertoire of narrative writing skills. When they wrote personal narratives, you expected five- to seven-page full-size booklets with pictures and quite a lot of writing on each page. You wanted children to tell the stories of single significant events, using words thoughtfully, using dialogue, and considering the audience. Now you need to continue to develop children's abilities to plan their stories before they start to write them. Build on prior narrative writing by addressing the concept of dramatic tension and by teaching children how to describe a problem in detail and experiment with how time passes in a story. Continue to stress planning stories before starting to write them, reducing the support you give and increasing the amount of independence you expect, thereby moving a little closer to your intended outcomes.

■ Overview

This unit takes about four weeks and, like the personal narrative unit, begins with a few days of oral storytelling. You will also spend some time describing realistic fiction situations and helping children come up with ideas for stories. At the end of this week, children will again publish a story by telling it orally as they turn the pages of a book in which they've written a brief synopsis of each part of the story. These written prompts help them remember key events or details in the story as they retell it but do not replace the oral retelling. Then they move on, transferring the oral story plans to full-size paper, using narrative development strategies to elaborate on and enrich their stories. You'll also teach children how to build some dramatic tension by slowing down the passage of time at strategic points in their stories.

■ Goals

The goals for this unit mostly have to do with planning and structuring narratives. Children will need good raw material—interesting subjects—from which to craft clear and engaging stories. You will also continue to develop their sense of community and encourage them to build more good writing habits.

Writing Quality

Children will:

- Write engaging narratives about realistic characters.

- Include a realistic problem and solution in each story.

- Use a variety of kinds of sentences.

- Show, not tell, characters' feelings.

- Think about which words to use to say exactly what they mean to say.

Writing Habits

Children will:

- Tell stories that have significance.

- Reread their stories often, thinking about how best to tell them.

- Revise their work as they write, not just in the revision section of the unit.

Writing Conventions

Children will:

- Learn to use quotation marks properly.

- Spell about a hundred frequently used words correctly.

Community

Children will:

- Be aware of which stories many of their peers have chosen to tell or write.

- Be able to make some smart decisions about which peers to ask for help with what aspect of writing.

- Suggest possible passages from books for classmates to use as mentor texts.

■ Getting Ready to Teach

As always, get ready to teach the unit by reviewing your assessments of the children and by preparing the lessons and materials they will need to succeed.

Considering the Students

Taking a look at the prior unit's assessment notes will help you focus on what children still need to work on. Pay special attention to any difficulties children had with the process of planning, telling, and writing stories. If necessary, plan to move more slowly through these steps.

Children who have written nicely focused personal narratives without much elaboration or development and who use only simple sentences will need help (in conferences or small-group minilessons) in developing their stories across a few pages while maintaining that focus. Children who have written narratives with too many things going on will need extra support in focusing their stories before they even begin writing.

Children who need support in building good habits as writers may need specific help putting their ideas into words. The writing habit you want to develop in this unit is communicating clearly with an audience. This concept may still be difficult for some children. They may see writing as something to put on a piece of paper and forget about, rather than as something that carries meaning from one person to another. Read their writing often and help them read their own writing critically. Ask them, "Is this what you mean to say? Is this what you want people to know? Is this how you want your story to be told?" and teach them to ask these questions of themselves.

Goals for developing community in this unit focus on collaboration. Children who may not have been fully involved with the work of the class will need extra encouragement and demonstrations of how to give and receive comments about writing and how to participate in discussions about literature. Make sure to ask for their input often, whether their hand is raised or not. You want them to know that they are expected to be part of the community and that their ideas are valuable.

If children are having a hard time grasping the conventions you expect them to learn, provide extra practice outside the writing workshop. Interactive writing, shared reading, and word study are ideal venues for focusing on these skills. The more they practice them, the better they will get at using them in the context of writing workshop.

Gathering Books

You can use many of the same books you used in the personal narrative unit, but you should also introduce (or return to) some other books. In particular, bring out a couple of books that have a clear problem and solution, like *It's MY Birthday!* by Pat Hutchins. And remember—you still want the books to be types of stories you can imagine your students writing.

After you have identified several things you can teach in each of the books you have chosen, jot the specific passages and the related strategies, techniques, or qualities of good writing down on sticky notes and place them inside the back covers of the books. Also think ahead about the things that might be challenging for children in this unit. Make specific notes about leads and endings, how problems are described and developed, and how writers resolve their problems. A list of suggested books is included in Appendix A.

Making Paper

Children can again use three-box paper to plan their fiction stories. Teach them early on to think of the boxes as setting the scene and introducing the characters, giving the characters a problem, and solving the problem. If they start with this well-defined story skeleton, they can develop it using what they know about the writer's craft, and their details will support the meaning of the story rather than be just decoration. When they are comfortable using three-box paper this way, have them use the same paper to develop the problems in their stories. All three boxes are now a place to stretch out how the trouble happens. Demonstrate this for them with an example of a simple story you have written.

When they are ready to write their stories in full detail based on the plans they have made, provide the same horizontal and vertical full-sheet writing paper they used for their personal narratives. Both kinds of paper have room for a picture and words, and children can choose the one they prefer.

■ Teaching

This unit follows a path similar to the personal narrative one. You'll look more closely at the story element of problem and solution and teach children to build dramatic tension by writing about this element in more detail. Your work with developing plot reinforces and extends what you've taught your students about writing personal narrative. As always, mentor texts will be integral to your work. Figure 5.1 shows the unit at a glance.

Reading Like Writers

This unit focuses on a couple of specific ways in which authors write fiction. I choose books with clear and realistic problems and solutions because I want the children to include problems and solutions they truly understand in their own fiction. To help them do this, I ask them to look specifically at this element when they begin to read the stories as writers, and together we construct a chart of various problems and solutions (see Figure 5.2).

Soon after starting this chart, I have the children brainstorm a list of realistic problems that could happen to them (see Figure 5.3). This gets them thinking about problems they have actually experienced (and therefore can write about in greater detail and with more honesty); later the list becomes a resource for children who have trouble coming up with an idea.

Telling and Planning Stories

This unit begins with several days of telling stories. Work with the class on telling a story as a sequence of events with a plot and characters. While this storytelling work is similar to that in the personal narrative unit, you need to teach the

TIME (A GENERAL GUIDELINE)	SECTION OF STUDY	WHAT NEEDS TO BE DONE IN THIS SECTION? CHILDREN WILL:
Ongoing	Reading Like Writers	• Discuss how some of their favorite stories are written and structured. • Categorize the kinds of trouble or problems dealt with in these stories. • Look at story leads.
4–5 days	Telling and Planning Stories	• Invent characters sort of like themselves. • Create a chart of everyday problems from which they may choose ideas for stories if they need to. • Practice telling the story as a sequence of events with a central plot line. • Revise how they tell the story by telling different parts with varying amounts of detail. • Give feedback to storytellers and accept feedback from listeners (mostly classmates) about how to make the story more engaging. • Accompany a book containing a small amount of text with an oral telling of the story.
7–8 days	Putting Our Stories into Writing	• Make plans for a few stories, using sketches and oral storytelling. • Use these plans to help write the stories. • Stretch the middle parts of their stories using dialogue, internal thinking, a description of the setting, or other qualities of good writing. • Study and categorize the endings in published books, using what they learn to improve the endings of their own books. • Try some writing elements that they have noticed in published books. • Add to the fiction writing decisions chart, noticing which students in the class have tried different techniques.
4–5 days	Revising and Editing	• Choose a story to publish. • Revise the story using the revision strategies checklist, including one new item: trying out different beginnings, or leads. • Edit the story using the editing strategies checklist.
2–3 days	Publishing	• Celebrate!

Figure 5.1 *Realistic Fiction at a Glance*

children some new skills for writing fiction. When they wrote personal narrative, they had great believable characters (themselves) and great realistic plots (their memories). With fiction, they have to make these things up. Of course, you want them to make them up well, so you need to do some thoughtful teaching. Remind the children of some of the essential things that stories have: characters, setting, and a plot with a problem that gets solved. (I remind them that some great stories don't have a problem that gets solved, but that the ones they are going to read and learn from all do, so the ones they write probably will too.)

For now, ask them to invent characters sort of like themselves. I say, "I am not going to write a story about an old Norwegian sailor because I don't know a single thing about old Norwegian sailors. Instead, my character is going to be a

TITLE	KIND OF TROUBLE	SOLUTION	HAVE ANY OF US TRIED THIS KIND OF STORY?
I'm Not Invited? by Diana Cain Bluthenthal	Character feels left out.	Character runs into her friend and discovers it is just a misunderstanding.	
A Weekend with Wendell, by Kevin Henkes	Friends are not getting along.	Sophie stands up for herself. Wendell decides to let her be in charge sometimes. They figure out how to take turns.	
Sing Out, Irene, by James Marshall	Character has to do something she does not want to do.	Irene decides to do her best even though she has a bad part in the play. She still acts in a way that she can be proud of.	
It's MY Birthday! by Pat Hutchins	Character does not want to share.	Billy has to ask his friends to play games with him because you can't play games by yourself. One of his friends is nice to him, even though Billy has been selfish. He learns that you have more fun when you share.	
Peter's Chair, by Ezra Jack Keats	Character does not want to share. Character does not like the change caused by a new sibling.	Peter has to go off by himself and be angry for a while. Then he accepts that Susie is his sister and she is there to stay. He decides to share his chair and to help his dad paint it pink for her.	
Wilson Sat Alone, by Debra Hess	New boy does not know how to make friends. The other kids think he does not want to make friends.	New girl comes along and shows everybody how to make friends by including Wilson in her game.	
The Pigeon Finds a Hot Dog! by Mo Willems	Character does not want to share.	The pigeon realizes he can get the duckling off his back by sharing the delicious hot dog.	
Julius, Baby of the World, by Kevin Henkes	Character does not like the change caused by a new sibling.	When her cousin calls the baby "disgusting," Lilly realizes she loves Julius after all.	

Figure 5.2 *Problems and Solutions in Realistic Fiction*

Everyday Problems

Mom said no.
My sister (brother, cousin, etc.) is bothering me.
I overslept.
I had to stay home sick.
I got lost in the store (park, zoo, etc.).
My hair looks funny.
Kids are teasing me.
There's only one ice cream (toy, sweater, etc.) left and we both want it.

Figure 5.3 *Everyday Problems for Realistic Fiction*

girl, because I am a girl, and she's going to play soccer, because I know a lot about soccer." This is enough to get them going in a fruitful direction. You can teach them more about character development later in the unit.

Next, you need to open the can of worms called *plot*. Plot is hard to explain to young children, except as "the stuff that happens in the story." Sometimes I say *plot* is "the things the characters do or the things that happen to them." Wrapped up in all of this is the problem–solution element. In order to get children to craft plots around realistic and believable problems, you first need to investigate the kinds of problems dealt with in your carefully preselected books. When children have trouble thinking of ideas—and more important, when they insist they really did get into a fiery crash at the NASCAR Classic—refer them to the chart of problems they created earlier and point out the everydayness of these problems.

Have each child make a small booklet, three pages with just a few words on each page, to accompany her or his retelling of the story. These pages are represented by the three boxes on their planning paper: setting the scene, the problem, and the solution. (See the example in Figure 5.4.) When this is clear, teach them to stretch the middle box, the problem, across the boxes of another sheet of planning paper (see Figure 5.5). This will support them as they learn to plan and write longer stories. The booklets help children remember the structure of the story so that they can tell it pretty much the same way every time they share it.

Possible Teaching Points

- *When we start to plan stories, we can invent characters sort of like ourselves and get them into trouble.* What's important here is that children work with characters that resemble themselves. Since they are writing realistic fiction, their characters need to be authentic and believable. Knowing characters well makes it easier to decide what kind of trouble they might get into and how they will respond to it when they do.

- *Now that we know what problems our characters will face, we can tell that part of the story in greater detail.* The model story (Figure 5.4) states the problem in simple language ("Christina got lost."). Demonstrate how to tell the story in more detail (Figure 5.5) by saying more about it ("She saw a butterfly and walked over to have a closer look. When she turned around, she couldn't see her parents anywhere. She was lost."). Think aloud about how the character can get lost in a way that makes sense: "It won't be very interesting if she suddenly gets lost for no reason; I have to find a way for her to get lost."

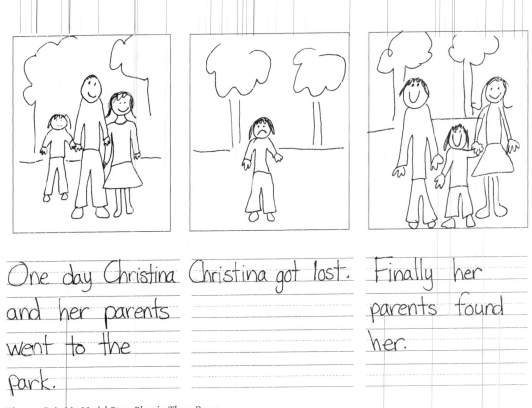

One day Christina and her parents went to the park.

Christina got lost.

Finally her parents found her.

Figure 5.4 *My Model Story Plan in Three Boxes*

- *Our stories are about made-up characters, so we should call them* **he or she, not I.** Much good fiction is written in first person. Here, though, you want children to write in the third person so the distinction between the writer and the character is clear. This will help them invent parts of the story even though they might have started from an idea that really happened. Making the change from *I, me,* or *my* to *she, her,* or *hers* is simple. Remembering they are allowed to make up details for the story may be harder. In your lessons and conferences, demonstrate (in your own writing) how you keep your characters like yourself but play around with them almost like playing with dolls—inventing their reality and circumstances, but having them respond as you yourself might.

Putting Our Stories into Writing

In this section, students continue to practice telling stories across their fingers and making plans for their stories. They begin turning their plans into written stories by using each box of the plan as a foundation for a page in a full-size (8½-by-11-inch) book. Most of your teaching, as in the personal narrative unit, will

She saw a butter-
fly and walked
over to have a
closer look.

When she turned
around, she
couldn't see her
parents anywhere.

She was lost.

Figure 5.5 *My Model Story Problem Stretched Across Three Boxes*

be about qualities of good writing. In particular, you'll teach them how to build some dramatic tension in their stories by telling the problem part of each story for a longer time.

The following are possible ways to develop, or stretch, stories:

- Add characters' thoughts or feelings.

- Include what characters see, hear, smell, taste, and feel.

- Let the reader hear characters talking (dialogue).

- Give a blow-by-blow account (tell everything that happened in a part of the story).

- Find the most important part, or heart, of the story and say more about it.

- Make sure details that are in the pictures are also in the words (for example, if characters are smiling in the picture, write that in the words too).

- Add a new beginning or ending.

- Tell about the setting.

Possible Teaching Points

- *Writers can show, not tell, their characters' problems (by using dialogue or describing action).* Return to your model story and demonstrate how to show, rather than tell, how the character got into the predicament. Do this by having the character talk or think to herself and by describing her actions ("She saw a butterfly fluttering nearby. 'How beautiful,' she thought. She walked over to have a closer look. She bent down and put out her finger. 'Mom, Dad,' she called, 'come look at this!' There was no answer. 'Mom? Dad?' She started to look in every direction. How would she find them?") Although you may be tempted to add more details, such as how the character felt or how she began to try to solve her problem, you'll have to wait. Describing the action and including dialogue are plenty for the children to learn in one lesson.

- *Sometimes writers let their readers know what their characters are thinking or feeling in their stories.* Again, model this yourself, thinking aloud as you write about what the character might be thinking, wondering, or feeling. ("She saw a butterfly fluttering nearby. 'How beautiful,' she thought. She walked over to have a closer look. She bent down and put out her finger. She hoped the butterfly would land on it. Maybe if she waited long enough it would. 'Mom, Dad,' she called, 'come look at this!' There was no answer. 'Mom? Dad?' She started to look in every direction. She wondered where they had gone. How would she find them? She sat down and began to cry.") The text is starting to sound fancy, and may be above the children's level of ability. It's important to add only one aspect or quality of good writing in each lesson. You haven't gone from "Christina was lost" to the previous text in just one lesson. To avoid getting too fancy, use a piece of one of your students' writing in some of your demonstrations.

- *Writers can make their stories more fun to listen to by making the problem last longer.* Teach children how to delay the solution by describing things the character might do to try to solve the problem or the things she sees or thinks about while she has the problem. ("Soon she had an idea. She remembered that when you get lost, you should stay in one place. She decided to stay exactly where she was. She hoped that if she waited long enough her parents would come back for her. She was worried, but she believed that they would come back. She saw a man and a woman come around the corner. Was it her parents? No, her mother had on a purple sweater.") Break this down into three separate lessons if it feels as if it's too much for one: describing what the character does to try solve the problem, describing what the character thinks of the problem, and telling what the character sees or hears while dealing with the problem.

- *Writers can make their readers feel as if they are in the story by showing them what the characters see.* Show your students how to add to the setting and scene of the story by describing what the character sees ("She looked around. Everywhere she looked she saw little girls happily holding their parents' hands.") Think aloud about how you don't want to describe every single thing the character might see but just those things that contribute to the character's feelings about her predicament.

- *Problems in realistic stories usually get solved by characters, not by magic.* Sometimes children have a lot of fun and success developing their problems but are not sure how to bring the whole thing home. I have seen the most engaging stories suddenly end with "And then they made up and everything was OK." What a letdown! I want to see the character *earn* her resolution. I explain all this to the children, asking them how they would like it if my story ended with the girl's parents just appearing out of nowhere. I then demonstrate how my story can end in a more rewarding way ("She wanted to leave her spot and go looking for her parents, but she knew if she just stayed put they'd be back. Just when she was beginning to lose hope, she saw the purple sweater coming around the corner. It was her mother! Her waiting paid off. She ran to her parents and gave them a big hug.")

- *Our stories need just one problem and one solution.* Some children will want to create many problems for their characters to face. This usually happens because the writer is trying to make his story really exciting for the reader. It is a sweet gesture and deserves to be complimented. After that, show the writer a book or two in which the author makes the story exciting within an economy of plot. In *Shortcut,* there is only one problem, but it sure is exciting. How does Donald Crews do it? He starts the story in the middle of the action, he includes the sounds the characters hear, he includes dialogue, and he builds suspense by telling the trouble part of the story in great detail. You have probably taught all of these things, so in a conference you can encourage a child to try one or two of them.

- *Our stories do need a problem.* The opposite of the previous issue is that some children may not have a problem in their stories. Does the writer think there is a problem? If she does, help her describe it more clearly in her writing, perhaps using action or dialogue. If she doesn't, support her in using the chart of everyday problems as a resource for ideas. Then again, maybe the story is more deliciously subtle than the typical problem–solution narrative. Maybe the writer has given her character an obstacle, a quest, or a challenge instead of a problem. (For example, entering a contest is not a problem, but it does create dramatic tension.) Help the writer work with this kind of plot element the same way you would help her handle a problem and its solution; you may also want her to describe how the character changes as a result of the experience.

Revising and Editing

While some children will no doubt have begun revising and editing their stories before now, at this point you'll make sure everyone is doing so and teach the class some new strategies. In the last unit, you taught them the importance of strong endings. Now add beginnings, or leads. Invite the children to join you in investigating the different sorts of beginnings and endings in your mentor stories (see Figure 5.6): great authors have great ways to draw readers into the worlds of their stories from the very beginning and to allow readers to leave those worlds with a sense of closure.

Rather than teach a new editing lesson, remind children to use the editing checklist, item by item. They may have checked the word wall for words and capitalization, but did they check punctuation and the spelling of known blends and digraphs?

Possible Teaching Points

- *One way to revise is to try a different beginning.* You looked at how stories begin earlier in the unit, and most children have probably tried to begin their stories based on what they noticed. Demonstrate trying out two or three different beginnings so that they can see how it works. (I do this orally first and then jot the beginnings on sticky notes and paste them right on the page.) You can start with dialogue ("'Mom? Dad?' Where were they? She had turned away for only a second."), setting the scene ("It was the first day of summer vacation. Christina was excited to be outside for a change."), or right in the middle of the action ("Christina felt the butterfly whoosh past her nose and began to run after it.").

- *Writers can help one another with editing.* It can be easier to look at someone else's work than at your own, especially when you have been working on it for a long time. Help some partners edit each other's work. Teach them

TITLE	WHAT KIND OF BEGINNING DOES THIS BOOK HAVE?	HOW DOES THIS BOOK END?	HAVE ANY OF US TRIED THESE THINGS?
I'm Not Invited? by Diana Cain Bluthenthal	Dialogue: "'What time is the party?' Kathleen said to Charles."	Dialogue: "Minnie smiled big. 'Me too!' she said."	
A Weekend with Wendell, by Kevin Henkes	Sets the scene: "On Friday afternoon, Wendell's parents dropped him off at Sophie's house."	Dialogue (sort of): "It was a note from Sophie. It said, 'I HOPE I SEE YOU SOON!'"	
Sing Out, Irene, by James Marshall	Sets the scene: "One after-noon in spring, Irene came home from school with tears in her eyes."	Tells how the character changed.	
It's MY Birthday! by Pat Hutchins	Sets the scene: "It was Billy's birthday."	Tells how the character changed: "And he shared his cake with everyone."	
Peter's Chair, by Ezra Jack Keats	Watches the character: "Peter stretched as high as he could. There! His tall building was finished."	Dialogue that shows how the character changed: "'Daddy,' said Peter, 'let's paint the little chair pink for Susie.' And they did."	

Figure 5.6 *Beginnings and Endings in Realistic Fiction*

to be gentle with each other, yet thorough. Rather than let them write on each other's paper, have them mark errors or raise questions on small sticky notes. Show them how to read a friend's writing once for meaning and again for conventions (correct spelling, punctuation, letter formation, and case).

Tiffany has incorporated several strategies from this unit into her story *Left Behind* (see Figure 5.7; Figure 5.8 details how she has used these strategies). Her work may help you see how your lessons will play out in your students' writing.

Publishing

Some teachers like to make this publication a big deal, since it is the last—and probably best—work the children will do this year. If you want to go all out, laminate and spiral-bind the pages, or have children create extra-special illustrations in art class, using fancier materials than usual.

However, if the celebration for the prior unit of study was big and special, make this one more intimate. It's nice to give everyone a chance to read his or her whole story. Since this takes a while, have four or five children read their stories to the class at the end of each day during the final week. After the children have read, toast them with little cups of juice and compliment the writers on specific things they have done well in their stories.

One sunny day, Mariah was riding her bike. There were big bumps in the road. It was hard to ride on. She was the slowest one.

She fell and got a cut. Everybody was ahead.

Figure 5.7 *Tiffany's Book,* Left Behind

She was lost. She didn't know where to go. She was scared.

Her knee was scraped. It was bleeding a lot. It hurt.

Figure 5.7 *(continued)*

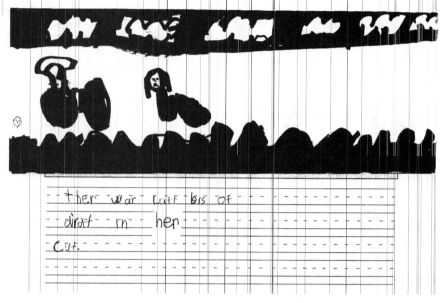

There were little bits of dirt in her cut.

She was scared because she thought that nobody would come back for her. It was scary.

Figure 5.7 *Tiffany's Book,* Left Behind *(continued)*

She stayed there for a couple of hours. She was thinking that they would come back if she had waited there long enough.

Her heart was beating very fast. But then her uncle came back for her.

Figure 5.7 *(continued)*

WRITING STRATEGY	HOW IT APPEARS IN TIFFANY'S STORY
Try making a fiction story from something that happened to you.	*Tiffany originally wrote most of this story about herself. She has added some details to this version and changed 'I' and 'my' to she and her.*
Tell about the setting.	There were bumps in the road. It was hard to ride on.
Add what the character thinks or wonders.	She was scared because she thought nobody would come back for her. She was thinking that they would come back if she had waited there long enough.
Add characters' feelings.	She was scared.
Show, not tell, feelings.	Her heart was beating very fast.
Find the most important part, or heart, of the story and say more about it.	Her knee was scraped. It was bleeding a lot. It hurt. There were little bits of dirt in her cut.
Add a new beginning or ending.	One sunny day Mariah was riding her bike.

Figure 5.8 How Tiffany Uses the Strategies She Has Learned

▥ Predictable Problems

When things go wrong, it does not mean we are not doing a good job. We just need to determine the cause of the problem and address it. Some issues that are common in this unit and possible ways to address them follow.

PROBLEM	WHAT IT LOOKS LIKE	POSSIBLE SOLUTION/ CONFERENCE
Children's stores are dull.	• Children write the plots of movies they have seen or video games they enjoy. • They choose characters very different from themselves and have trouble writing about them authentically. • Children tell stories in which nothing really happens.	Children sometimes believe these are the only things worth telling stories about. They need to be reminded that their own lives can be the inspiration for their fiction. Speak to them as if their lives are what really matters in this classroom. Sometimes if you let a child write one of these stories, he gets it out of his system and can move on to more fertile ground. Choose stories to read aloud to children that validate the importance of things that really happen in their lives.

Children don't yet have a strong grasp of how good fiction works.	• The story is one long sentence with a lot of "and then . . . and then . . ." language. • There are many problems and no solution. • The story keeps on going after the problem is solved and a resolution is reached. • There is a lot of detail but not much substance.	Have lots of published books on hand as visions for how children's books can look. Read aloud good stories throughout the unit, pointing out how authors have avoided common pitfalls. Teach minilessons that deal explicitly with these issues. Children usually do things in their fiction writing because they think these things are going to make the story good, not (as it sometimes seems) to irritate us. Help them by working *with* them, not against them.
Your teaching is not reaching all learners.	• More advanced students do not appear to be working at their full potential. • Struggling students seem unengaged.	Make sure your mentor texts are appropriate for the range of ability levels in your class. Confer with these children a few extra times; they may need more individualized teaching until they have a better idea of what they can expect from themselves.

■ Assessment

At the end of the unit, it's time to look over the work and compare what you see with what you hoped you would see. Because it is the last unit of the year, the assessment rubric (see Figure 5.9) incorporates the goals for the whole year, not just those for the unit. You probably will not be able to use this information to inform your future teaching with these same children. Nevertheless, you will be able to reflect on how your attention to text structure helped the overall quality of your students' writing. What you discover will influence how you incorporate planning and organization, or *structure*, into your curriculum in the years to come.

WRITING QUALITY	1 RARELY	2 SOMETIMES	3 MOST OF THE TIME	4 MORE THAN I EXPECT
Child chooses topics that matter deeply to him/her.	❏	❏	❏	❏
Child's writing is planned and organized for clarity.	❏	❏	❏	❏
Child makes decisions about how to structure her/his writing for maximum effect.	❏	❏	❏	❏
Child tries a variety of genres or forms in his/her writing.	❏	❏	❏	❏
Child uses a variety of kinds of sentences.	❏	❏	❏	❏
Child thinks about which words to use to say exactly what she/he means to say.	❏	❏	❏	❏
Child understands that writing is meant to be read and has a job of communicating something to an audience.	❏	❏	❏	❏

WRITING HABITS

	1 RARELY	2 SOMETIMES	3 MOST OF THE TIME	4 MORE THAN I EXPECT
Child tells stories that have significance and are engaging.	❏	❏	❏	❏
Child plans work before starting to write.	❏	❏	❏	❏
Child reads and rereads his/her writing, thinking about how best to tell what he/she wishes to say.	❏	❏	❏	❏
Child tries writing techniques she/he has seen in books.	❏	❏	❏	❏
Child has a vision for how he/she wants his/her story to go and revises often to achieve this.	❏	❏	❏	❏
Child thinks of herself/himself as a writer with a message.	❏	❏	❏	❏
Child has developed and maintains a daily habit of writing quietly.	❏	❏	❏	❏
Child sees writing possibilities everywhere (even at recess!).	❏	❏	❏	❏

COMMUNITY

	1 RARELY	2 SOMETIMES	3 MOST OF THE TIME	4 MORE THAN I EXPECT
Child is aware of which topics many of his/her peers have chosen.	❏	❏	❏	❏
Child is able to make some smart decisions about which peers to ask for help with different writing issues.	❏	❏	❏	❏
Child shares books and observations about books with classmates.	❏	❏	❏	❏
Child asks questions about and compliments classmates' work.	❏	❏	❏	❏
Child cares about environment and supplies and treats them with care.	❏	❏	❏	❏

WRITING CONVENTIONS

	1 RARELY	2 SOMETIMES	3 MOST OF THE TIME	4 MORE THAN I EXPECT
Child uses learned punctuation correctly.	❏	❏	❏	❏
Child forms letters correctly and in the proper case.	❏	❏	❏	❏
Child spells correctly about one hundred frequently used words.	❏	❏	❏	❏

Figure 5.9 *End-of-Year Assessment Rubric*

Conclusion

As a classroom teacher and now as a staff developer, I have found that a little attention to structure can lift the quality of student writing dramatically. The structures in this book are a few of many that young writers can use to communicate more clearly. Studying these, you will begin to notice the many ways writers choose to organize their thoughts. You will no doubt bring other mentor texts to your students' attention. Pamphlets, children's periodicals like *Time for Kids,* letters, instruction manuals—any good writing has structures that children can study and use in their own writing.

For me as a teacher of reading and writing, the purpose of literature is to share experiences and knowledge—to forge connections among the citizens of our world. The meaning a writer and her reader make together is greater than the meaning either makes alone. When we teach children to plan and organize their ideas, we empower them to become meaning makers, sharers of ideas, and active participants in the world of communication.

For more information visit my website at www.StephanieParsons.com

Appendix A: Suggested Mentor Texts

Pattern Books

A Party, by Joy Cowley. A list of items that go together to make a party. Good for introducing pattern books in their simplest form.

If You Meet a Dragon . . . , by Joy Cowley. All the parts of a dragon you can tickle to make him go away. The pattern is maintained throughout the book until the last page, which is a different kind of sentence. Good for teaching how to change the pattern on the last page of a book.

Where Does a Leopard Hide? by Paul Reeder. All the pages follow the pattern "A _____ hides in the _____." Beginning with a leopard, the book lists where different kinds of animals hide. A helpful mentor text for children who want to write nonfiction.

Things That Make You Feel Good, Things That Make You Feel Bad, by Todd Parr. A list of things that make you feel good and bad. The pattern is a seesaw, with the pages alternating between good and bad. Good example of writing about opposites.

Our Granny, by Joy Cowley. Funny things the grandmother does. The pattern is "When she plays, she plays," and so on. The last page extends the pattern. Can be a good example of ways to add information to a book.

Worm Is Stuck, by Kathy Caple. Worm gets into all kinds of shapes, then gets stuck in a knot. Good for showing how a pattern can describe action or tell about an event. This book is part of a set of four from the Brand New Readers imprint at Candlewick Press.

Water Changes, by Brenda Parkes. Nonfiction. The first page introduces the concept that water changes; then the pattern addresses the things that water can change into. The last page asks a question. Good for teaching children how to leave their readers thinking about the topic even after finishing the book.

My Friends, by Taro Gomi. A list of the things the narrator has learned from different friends. The pattern is: "I learned to jump from my friend the dog." The last page has a slight twist. Shows how children might use more words even while they adhere closely to a pattern in their writing.

When I Was Little, by Jamie Lee Curtis. A list that contrasts the past and present by seesawing back and forth between a description of what the narrator was like when she was little and how she is different now. Helpful for teaching children how to use a pattern to point out differences between two things.

When I Was Five, by Arthur Howard. Two lists. The first describes how the narrator was when he was five, the second describes how he is different now that he is six. Both lists have the same last item, and the book ties them together: "Some things never change." Good mentor text for children who want to highlight differences *and* similarities.

Earrings! by Judith Viorst. A repeated refrain heightens the emotional intensity of a child's diatribe about how badly she needs to have pierced ears. Good for showing how to use a refrain to remind readers of an important message.

The Moon Was Best, by Charlotte Zolotow. A language pattern in the middle is bookended by narrative at the very beginning and end. Nice example of a pattern that tells a story.

When I Was Young in the Mountains, by Cynthia Rylant. Memoir. The first sentence on each page begins "When I was young in the mountains" and goes on to describe an incident from the author's childhood. Good for teaching children how to use this text structure to string together scenes with a common theme.

Nonfiction

What's Inside? by Colin Walker and *Baby Animals at Home,* by Miriam Frost. Relatively easy reading level. Different questions followed by different answers. Good introductions to the structure.

Where Are the Seeds? by Pauline Cartwright and *Seeds, Seeds, Seeds,* by Brian and Jillian Cutting. Same question repeated with different answers. Good examples of showing how similar things can be so different.

What Does a Garden Need? by Judy Nayer, *What Can Fly?* by Brenda Parkes, *What Lays Eggs?* by Katherine Gracestone, and *Who Beats the Heat?* (about desert animals), by Pamela Chanko and Daniel Moreton. One question with many answers. Good for teaching about different aspects of a single concept, quality, or place.

Grow, Seed, Grow, by Lisa Trumbauer. Describes the life cycle of a plant. One question answered by rest of book. Good example for children who want to write at length on one idea.

Will We Miss Them? Endangered Species, by Alexandra Wright, *What's Under the Log?* by Anne Hunter, and *What's in the Pond?* by Anne Hunter. Different questions with different long answers. Good mentor books for children who are able to write longer pieces.

Personal Narratives

Note: Some of these are fiction written in the first person.

Shortcut, by Donald Crews. The kids take a shortcut along the railroad tracks when they should have taken the road. After a big fright, they learn never to take the shortcut again. Nice example of building tension and showing action through use of dialogue.

The Hating Book, by Charlotte Zolotow. A big misunderstanding almost ruins a friendship, but when the girls finally talk, they work out their problem. Good for teaching about adding the characters' thoughts and feelings to help tell the story.

No More Kissing! by Emma Chichester Clark. Momo, a young monkey, cannot understand why everyone thinks kissing is so great. When his baby brother will not stop crying, though, Momo "accidentally" kisses him and finds that it is not so bad after all.

A Chair for My Mother, by Vera B. Williams. Family members work together and save money to buy a comfortable new chair for the mother after a fire destroys their home. Great examples of time moving slowly and quickly to show importance.

Fireflies! by Julie Brinckloe. After catching fireflies on a summer night, a boy discovers that setting something free is better than keeping it in a jar. Illuminates the character's internal struggle. Also good for teaching the use of clear and specific language.

Realistic Fiction

Sing Out, Irene, by James Marshall. Irene gets cast as the toadstool in the school play and is unhappy with such an unglamorous role. She finds a way to play her part with pride, though. Good examples of showing emotions rather than just telling about them.

It's MY Birthday! by Pat Hutchins. Billy does not want to share any of his new birthday presents with his friends. When he opens a present he cannot play with alone, his friends are off playing together. He has to find a way to share. Good for showing how a repeated refrain can help move the story along.

Peter's Chair, by Ezra Jack Keats. A new baby in the house causes some problems for Peter. He learns to accept his new role as big brother. Good examples of showing emotions rather than just telling about them.

Big Sister and Little Sister, by Charlotte Zolotow. Big sister takes care of little sister and knows everything. When little sister decides she wants to do some things for herself, both have to learn to accept each other. Nice for showing perspectives of two characters, not just one main one.

The Kissing Hand, by Audrey Penn. Chester Raccoon is scared to go to school, so his mother shows him how to hold on to a safe and warm feeling while he is away from home. Some examples in which time is slowed down and a small moment is told in great detail.

I'm Not Invited? by Diana Cain Bluthenthal. Minnie hears that her best friend is having a party. She waits all week for an invitation that never comes. Just when she has reached the peak of her misery, she discovers that her best friend's *sister* is the one having the party, and that her best friend would rather be out having fun with Minnie. Good for showing how tension can be created by a character's thoughts and actions.

The Pigeon Finds a Hot Dog! by Mo Willems. Told through dialogue presented in speech bubbles. The pigeon finds a hot dog. The nudgy duckling keeps asking the pigeon questions about the delights of hot dogs until the pigeon, annoyed by the interruptions, decides to share. Great for demonstrating how dialogue can show action or move a story along.

Appendix B: Types Of Paper

- Four-Box Paper
- Two-Box Paper
- Story Paper
- Story-Planning Paper

FOUR-BOX PAPER

TWO-BOX PAPER

STORY PAPER

STORY-PLANNING PAPER

Units of Study for Primary Writing

A Yearlong Writing Curriculum for Grades K-2

Lucy Calkins and her colleagues from the Teachers College Reading and Writing Project have helped hundreds of thousands of teachers take their first forays into the teaching of writing. *Units of Study for Primary Writing* provides easy access to the magic of their teaching by presenting minute-by-minute, live-from-the-classroom coaching as they show you how to **take your children from oral and pictorial story telling, through emergent, and into fluent writing.**

Units of Study for Primary Writing / 9 Books + 1 CD-ROM / **$159.00** / 0-325-00604-0

Additional Resources for the Teaching of Primary Writers

Conferring with Primary Writers (CD-ROM) provides 61 elementary classroom conference transcripts in a concise, easy-to-read format — plus a nimble sorting feature allows you to modify and adapt transcripts into cutomized study guides.
61 modifiable conference transcripts / **$25.00** / 0-325-00638-5

Big Lessons from Small Writers (DVD) is a comprehensive, easy-to-navigate instructional resource that presents 22 video clips of Lucy and others teaching minilessons, conferences, and whole class shares — with optional voice-over coaching commentary from Lucy Calkins.
2 hours of instructional video clips / **$45.00** / 0-325-00748-9

To order or to sample these resources
www.unitsofstudy.com